TRACKING MACKENZIE TO THE SEA ∞

TRACKING MACKENZIE TO THE SEA

Coast to Coast in Eighteen Splashdowns

ROBERT J. HING

≈ Anchor Watch Press

Copyright © 1992 by Robert J. Hing
First published in 1992 by Anchor Watch Press
P.O. Box 1010, Manassas, Virginia 22110
ALL RIGHTS RESERVED

Publisher's Cataloging in Publication

Hing, Robert J.
   Tracking Mackenzie to the sea : coast to coast in eighteen
splashdowns / Robert J. Hing.
   p. cm.
   Includes bibliographical references and index.
   0-9631460-0-9
   1. North America—Description and travel. 2. Seaplanes. 3. Canoes and canoeing—North America. 4. Mackenzie, Alexander, 1763–1820. I. Title.
E41.H5 1992   970
91-77487

Grateful acknowledgement is made to the following for permission to quote material in copyright:

University of Toronto Press, for excerpts from *Fur Trade Canoe Routes of Canada/Then and Now* by Eric W. Morse, 2d ed. 1984, © 1979 Ministry of Supply and Services Canada; *The New Yorker,* for excerpts from "The Ancient Forest," © 1990 Catherine Caufield; Douglas & McIntyre, for excerpts from *The North West Company,* copyright © 1973 by Marjorie Wilkins Campbell; Sierra Club Books, for excerpts from *Magnetic North* by David Halsey, copyright © 1990; John Farquharson Ltd., New York, for excerpts from *The Lonely Sea and the Sky,* copyright © 1964 by Francis Chichester, (originally published by Hodder and Stoughton, London, reprinted by Paragon House, New York, 1990); for excerpts from *Ride on the Wind,* copyright © 1936 by Francis Chichester, © 1989 by Giles Chichester, (originally published by Hamish Hamilton, London, reprinted by Paragon House, New York, 1989).

Printed in the United States of America

9 8 7 6 5 4 3 2 1

To the memory of my uncle
Flying Officer Ronald Harrison, R.A.F.V.R.
Spitfire pilot
who trained at Medicine Hat, Alberta
was "shot up" while flying cover for the Canadian
Army's raid on Dieppe, August 19, 1942
and was killed later that same year

I wish to thank The National Geographic Society for the use of their library and map room; the Embassy of Canada, Washington, D.C., for access to their library; and the National Maritime Museum, Greenwich, England, for advice on Mackenzie's track and methods of eighteenth century navigation.

My thanks also to Mike Forster for introducing me to seaplaning; to Ed Kelly, of East Haddam, Connecticut, for a fine job repairing my float; and to the seaplaners everywhere I stopped, from Lake Chickamauga to Lake Whatcom. Free as a bird in the air, I was dependent upon their help as soon as I was on the water.

For editorial suggestions on streamlining the original manuscript, my thanks to Dana Rae Pomeroy, Sam Blate, and Carolyn Zimmerman.

Jay Frey, of the Edo Corporation, was kind enough to review the text and to clarify several technical points.

C·O·N·T·E·N·T·S

PREFACE: THE CANOE AND THE PONTOON XV

I PREPARATIONS

Waterborne   5

Decide to follow Mackenzie to the sea.   Learn water flying at Baltimore.   Acquire small floatplane at Chattanooga.   Fly it back without radio or compass.

Which way to the Coast?   15

Perplexities of charting Mackenzie's route to the Pacific.   Shortness of season and its effects.

Behind the Eight Ball   25

Make preparations for the voyage.   Encounter problems while fitting out.   A hole in the float, etc.   Dunked in Connecticut River.

II MACKENZIE'S TRACK

Days 1–5   39

Arrival outside Montreal.   Go into the city.   Pick up the trail of Mackenzie and the voyageurs.   Embark on the St. Francis River and proceed along the Ottawa.   Arrival at Trout Lake.   Grounded there

x · CONTENTS

by bad weather.   Hard lives of the inhabitants noted.   The fur business in North Bay collapsed.

Days 6–9   55

Renew my voyage.   Perils of a seaplane flight to Thunder Bay.   Fog along the coast.   Landing on Lake Superior in heavy swell, etc.   Visit Old Fort William, where the two ends of the Voyageurs' Highway met.   Grounded at Thunder Bay by weather.   Then by engine starter repair.   Singular conduct of the natives.   Chopping up a piano, etc.   Obliged to wait by the high wind.

The Canadian Shield   67

Necessary account of its importance to this route.

Days 10–12   73

Embark from Thunder Bay.   In danger of being lost over Lake du Bois, where the voyageurs frequently lost their way.   Land at Kenora.   Curious life styles reported there.   Unexpected stop-over at Riverton on the shore of Lake Winnipeg.   Weathered in.   Go sightseeing.   Visit to town of four dogs and a pickup truck.   Saw a white pelican.

Days 13–16   81

A near crack-up at Grace Lake.   Circumstances of it. Grounded for repairs.   Some account of The Pas. Visit to an Indian Reservation-cum-shopping center. Alarm and dissatisfaction at home.   Resume my voyage.   Reach Cumberland House.   Perplexities from the numerous lakes and the channels of rivers.

Unable to find Frog Portage.   Land on Lac La Ronge.

Days 17–20   95

Land at village of the natives, called Buffalo Narrows. Their information respecting the country.   Very blowing weather prevents my departure.   Fabulous tales of the natives.   Conduct and appearance of the inhabitants.   Meet with the Indians.

Days 21–23   107

To Fort Chipewyan via Methye Portage.   Fine view of the Clearwater River.   Land at Small Lake. Grounded by bad weather.   Some account of Fort Chip.   An allurement: "The only thing worth seeing at Fort Chip." Conference with the Indians.

Days 24–26   117

Leave Fort Chipewyan.   Proceed along the Peace River to Footner Lake.   Optimism of Canadian cartographers: old bath tub sole evidence for reputed town.   Come in sight of Rocky Mountains.   Take the wrong fork.   Alight on Tabor Lake.   Depart from there.   Arrive at an arm of the sea.   Fly over Bella Coola and down the wrong fiord.   Steer for the island of Bella Bella.

Days 27–30   145

Change the plan of my return.   Resolve to leave for Seattle but spooked by fog.   Congenial companions. Again endeavor to reach Vancouver Island.   Turned back by fog.   Warned against going inland. Success on third attempt.   Arrival over Vancouver

Island.   Curious appearance of deforested areas. Abundance of eagles at Campbell River noted. Become lost in the crowd at Friday Harbor.

The Return   *153*

Jet to the East Coast in 4 hrs. and 28 minutes.

III   PARTICULARS

The Crossing of North America   *157*

Mackenzie's feat in the context of his time.

Modern Canoe Crossings   *169*

Three narratives of uncommon physical exertion.

The Survival of the Beaver Hat   *173*

Profitable item that paid for the first crossing of North America, the beaver hat is still very much with us.

The Fur Trade: On the Skids   *179*

Past importance, present decline.

APPENDIX 183

Time and Distances flown 185
Equipment carried 186
Postscripts 188
French and the Indians since Mackenzie's Time 190

NOTES 195

SOURCES 209

INDEX 214

M · A · P · S

1. NORTH AMERICAN WATERWAYS TO
   THE PACIFIC OCEAN   frontispiece
   These people describe the distance across the country as very short to the Western Ocean. . . .

2. MONTREAL   44–45
   Leaving La Chine, they proceed to St. Ann's, within two miles of the Western extremity of the island of Montreal. . . .

3. MATTAWA RIVER TO GEORGIAN BAY   50–51
   Out of the Lake Nepisingui flows the Riviere de Francois.

4. LAKE SUPERIOR TO LAKE WINNIPEG   68–69
   In short, the country is so broken by lakes and rivers, that people may find their way in canoes in any direction they please.

5. CUMBERLAND HOUSE TO FROG PORTAGE   90–91
   . . . it is necessary to cross the Portage de Traite, or, as it is called by the Indians . . . the Portage of the Stretched Frog Skin.

6. METHYE PORTAGE   96–97
   This portage is the one that divides the waters which discharge themselves into Hudson's Bay, from those that flow into the Northern Ocean.

7. THE DIVIDE BETWEEN THE PEACE
   AND FRASER RIVERS   127
   *This [Arctic Lake] I consider as the highest and
   Southernmost source of the . . . Peace River.*

8. THE PACIFIC COAST   134–135
   *At about eight we got out of the river into an arm of
   the sea. The surrounding hills were involved in fog.*

P · R · E · F · A · C · E

The Canoe and the Pontoon

To retrace the route of Mackenzie's epic canoe journey with a pontoon-equipped airplane, as I did, and then to offer an account of it, requires some explanation as to my mode of transport. In the event, the trip itself sustained the notion of a small seaplane as an airborne canoe, one that on this excursion to the coast rarely rose farther from the water than the height of a small tower, and that carried me into contact with some, at least, of the essential experiences of Mackenzie's voyage—wind, waves, fog, mishaps of all kinds.

Although at first glance the noisy seaplane and the silent canoe may appear quite unlike, they share a number of characteristics, and differ only in certain respects.

Both operate with a minimum of supporting infrastructure (docks, canals, prepared runways).

Each is near to being an all-terrain vehicle. The canoe can be carried overland to useable water; the floatplane can traverse every sort of country, and then set down on any convenient stretch of water.

Neither can readily operate in high winds or waves.

The canoe, powered by human muscle, is constrained in its travels by available food sources; the floatplane, gasoline-powered, is dependent on fuel caches.

Both craft are vulnerable to damage.

In some respects, they are not similar. The canoe is more

easily repaired than the floatplane. Yet, the canoe is useless in winter. (The floatplane can be converted to skis.)

In Mackenzie's time, and long after, the bark canoe was state-of-the-art transportation for North America's inland waterways, both for the Indians and for the Europeans, who adopted the Indian canoe without change. Now, the essential role of the canoe—transport in a roadless country—has been taken over by the pontoon-equipped airplane, the floatplane. Today, the De Havilland Beaver and the De Havilland Otter are the working craft of the North, and the canoe—which itself is often transported by floatplane, lashed to the float struts—has been relegated to a recreational role.

The design of the bark canoe evolved over hundreds of years; that of the seaplane was developed very rapidly. Seven years after the Wrights first flew, and less than two years after they demonstrated their airplane in France, Henri Fabre flew his floatplane off the waters of the harbor at La Mède, near Marseille. (His plane is now in the museum at Chalais-Meudon outside Paris, with the placard, *C'est le premier hydravion du Monde.*)

Fabre's rickety airplane was a mid-wing canard, mounted on three small floats. Today's working seaplane is, often as not, a high-wing aircraft on two large pontoons. (This configuration is best adapted to coming alongside a dock. It also lessens the possibility of dragging a wing tip in the water.) The conventional modern pontoon, or float, is made of aluminum, 32/1000 inch thick (forty-thousandths on the bottom), and is a rigid structure with bulkheads and a keel, joined together by ten thousand rivets.

The structure of a bark canoe, having neither bulkheads nor keel, was an even more ingenious design than that of the modern airplane's pontoon. Without the bark cover in place, the greater part of the wooden structure of the bark canoe would collapse. In aeronautical parlance, it had a "stressed skin."

Each of the two EDO floats on my Cessna 140 displaced 1,650 lbs (more than the loaded weight of the airplane) and had six watertight compartments. The total installed weight of the two pontoons was a mere 208 lbs. (The EDO Corporation also built the floats for the Lockheed Sirius, which carried the Lindberghs across Canada to China in 1931, as recorded in Anne Morrow Lindbergh's fine book, *North to the Orient*. This airplane is exhibited at the National Air and Space Museum in Washington, D.C.)

A bark canoe was simple to build. Mackenzie's men, on an island in the Fraser River, built a canoe from materials at hand in four days, which the impatient Mackenzie thought too long a time. Similarly, the bark canoe was a lot more easily repaired than is an aluminum structure. In this respect, it was like a fabric-covered airplane—like the wings of my seaplane.

Aluminum pontoons and bark canoes have this in common: both are very vulnerable to damage, the bark canoe more so: McPhee, in his book *The Survival of the Bark Canoe*, reports, "landing, we are out of the canoes and in the water ourselves long before the bark can touch bottom. The Indians did just that. . . ."

TRACKING MACKENZIE TO THE SEA ≈

P·A·R·T I

Preparations

It was not so much the actual time required to learn water flying, acquire a seaplane, fit it out, and plan the route, as completing all the preparations in time for the short Northern season.

Mike Forster's Aeronca Chief seaplane at Back River, Maryland, October 14, 1988. Airplane has 85 h.p. engine, and is mounted on EDO 1400 floats. Trailer is for towing seaplane to and from beach. Note auxiliary fin, one on each tailplane, to maintain directional stability in flight, counteracting the extra side area of the floats ahead of the yaw axis of the airplane. The hydrodynamic step on the keel of each float helps break suction on take-off (an innovation by Glenn Curtiss in 1911). The water rudder at the end of the right float is in the retracted position.

Waterborne

🛶 . . . the 9th May 1793 I in a Bark Canoe left one of our settlements in the North West on the Unjigah or Peace River Latitude 56.9 North and longitude 117.43 West from Greenwich, for the purpose of penetrating to the Western Ocean. (*Alexander Mackenzie to John Simcoe, Lt.-Governor of Upper Canada, September 10, 1794*)

*I*n May 1988, Chuck Spinelli, an airport acquaintance of mine, mentioned that he had signed up for a seaplane course in Baltimore. "Why don't you join me?" he asked. Why would I go seaplaning? I wondered. Then my memory went back to the year before, beneath the ground, to the basement of the State Library at Richmond.

I had gone there to see a first edition copy of a book famous in its time, but now obscure. Upon my request, the librarian led me down two flights of narrow steps to the Rare Books Room. He unlocked the door, and switched on the lights. Then he searched the dimly-lit stacks, and brought out the book. It was a handsome volume, near to 8½ × 11 inches in size, and better laid out than most books of today. It recounted the story of an epic journey across North America by canoe. It was a story of discovery and adventure, of a vast country of lakes and rivers; and I was frankly fascinated.

Suddenly, I saw Chuck's invitation in a new light. The seaplane would provide a modern-day means for me to travel the almost-forgotten route of Mackenzie without having to paddle millions of strokes in a canoe. I would hop from lake to lake, river to river, clear across the continent, along the same watery highways travelled by Mackenzie and his voyageurs—

and the Indians before them. What perfect freedom it would be to splash down on any sunlit lake I chose along the way!

Only later did I have another realization: I might not be so well qualified for my venture as Mackenzie had been for his.

* * *

Viewed from an airplane over Baltimore, the layout of the surrounding country is obvious enough: the several rivers flowing into the Chesapeake Bay, and the Eastern Shore about ten miles away, connected to the mainland by the Bay Bridge. The layout of the country was not so obvious when I had to navigate my automobile through the tangle of highways around Baltimore on my first trip there. These cluttered highways were posted with a confusion of signs: "Bill's Carpets," "Highway 40 Next Exit," "Female Review," "Discount Mattress," "Sam's Diner," "Liquors," and—the one I was looking for—"Motel $27." The motel, in turn, had its own sign: "Due to continued driving-off without paying, we have to go with a pay-first policy."

Baltimore is the chief town of the Chesapeake, and home to the only seaplane base for miles around, located just north of the city, on Back River. Back River Neck is a heavily-wooded peninsula frequented by herons and ospreys; from a sandy beach on its shore you can look south across the river to the smokestacks of the Sparrows Point steel mill, and from this same beach, which adjoins an air strip, you can sometimes see seaplanes being launched onto the river, which is very wide at this point. Here I would learn the rudiments of flying a seaplane, a six-hour course of dual instruction splashing around on Back River, with occasional side trips to the nearby Severn River at Annapolis, in Mike Forster's little Aeronca floatplane.

Arriving at Back River, I saw the Aeronca parked, like a canoe out of water, on the grass in front of the flight office about five hundred yards from the river. Here it all was: the little craft, the river, and—to the west—all of North America.

No-one was around, and I took the time to look the airplane over. It was an uncomplicated machine. The only extra control that this small seaplane had, compared with the equivalent landplane, was a water rudder on the end of one of the two large pontoons. This water rudder evidently steered the seaplane when it taxied on the water at low speeds. The water rudder was operated by the same rudder bar in the cockpit which worked the air rudder, and it could be retracted by means of a spring-loaded handle. (Later, I learned that when the seaplane is drifted backwards, the water rudder should be retracted, or it will oppose the air rudder.)

Six hours instruction, I thought, would be ample for such a simple craft.

Mike Forster showed up and the course started immediately.

"Do you know how to handle a sailboat?"

"Yes."

"It's something like that."

He went off to the hangars behind the flight office, and came back with two helpers and four iron pipes (troublesome pipes, as I would later find out.)

The four of us were going to slide the seaplane down to the beach. ("She was so light," Mackenzie said of his canoe, "that two men could carry her on a good road three or four miles without resting.") No. We were going to load the seaplane onto a trailer, which was then to be towed by tractor down to the beach.

The procedure couldn't have been much more awkward if we had been transporting a baby whale. It consisted, basically, of backing the trailer up to the seaplane, placing the iron pipes crosswise on the bed of the trailer, then depressing the rear of the trailer, pushing down on the rear of the floats and—here came the hard part—pushing the plane uphill so that it rolled forward over the pipes onto the trailer.

Once at the beach, the trailer was backed into the water

until the plane floated free. The lines were then loosened from the bow cleats, and the trailer towed away.

"One thing about seaplanes," said Mike, "You're very dependent upon other people."

This did not seem to bother Mike. Benign of manner, prematurely white-haired (his flying career included dodging SAM missiles over Hanoi), Mike had graduated from the Naval Academy at Annapolis in the 1950's and now—the apple had not fallen far from the tree—he operated a seaplane school on Back River.

No wind sock was visible from the beach, and there were no marked runways on the water. The only signs, such as the red triangle on a stake at the end of the sand spit called Witchcoat Point, were intended for boat navigation. Just then a visiting seaplane landed out in the river beyond this point and taxied back towards us on the beach. The seaplane pilot didn't see the marker and plowed across the sand spit, which was under a few inches of water at the current state of the tide, with only a momentary shudder of the airplane. "He could have ripped the floats off," I suggested.

"That's why seaplane insurance is so high," said Mike. But he seemed more interested in the Chesapeake Bay Retriever that was seated next to the pilot of the incoming seaplane.

Which direction should we use for take-off? I looked at the smoke stacks on Sparrows Point but couldn't tell within 150 degrees where the wind was coming from. I pulled up a handful of grass and threw it in the air. The wind was southeast. Mike hand-cranked the prop (from the rear, standing on the right float), and then we taxied out into the middle of the river. Mike said, "Here's how to tell where the wind's from." He retracted the water rudder, and the little seaplane, lacking any keel, weathercocked directly into the wind.

"Let's take off," said Mike.

I pushed the throttle wide and started the plane across the water. I had flown little airplanes that practically jumped into the air, but this strange machine just vibrated along, threw up clouds of spray—and remained glued to the water. "The shore is coming up," I yelled at Mike.

"Hold her down," he said.

The plane picked up a little more speed, then, when Mike motioned me to relax the forward pressure on the yoke, the plane unstuck from the water and climbed slowly above the river bank.

"Seaplanes need *twice* the distance to take off," yelled Mike. I was to learn this lesson again, more forcibly, at a farther place.

We circled around and descended towards the river. "See those wind streaks on the water?" said Mike. By then, the engine was throttled back so it was easy to talk. The wind streaks were not lined up with our flight path. The wind had changed direction, and I was drifting sideways down to the water.

"See what I mean?" he said. We veered away from the water and made a fresh approach.

The final part of the seaplane curriculum (or arcanum, as I now thought of it) at Back River was "sailing." Sailing is the technique of reaching a desired point on the beach or dock in conditions of high wind, when the seaplane would be otherwise unmanageable—might flip over—by drifting the craft backwards or slantwise, never, like a sailboat, directly cross wind or down wind.

The useable part of the beach at Back River was fairly small and, with the wind blowing onshore so that one couldn't head directly towards it, it was a nice trick to track backwards to the beach. I would usually end up a hundred yards from my objective and have to motor out into the river and try again. It was in these conditions that the small seaplane demonstrated its essential unhandiness and revealed the need for yet-to-be-acquired skills to master it. Those skills, I realized, would have to be acquired "on the job," flying coast to coast.

If I expected to get some help from reading about the mysteries of flying a seaplane, I found little encouragement.

> On the water, a seaplane is a fast motor-boat as long as the propeller is turning, but as soon as the motor is cut it becomes a fast yacht, sailing down wind. Broadly speaking, in the air it has all the problems of an ordinary aeroplane, with a fresh set of problems and hazards on the water. It may drift fast on to a pier or a boat astern, and it has not the hardy construction of a yacht. A wing can crumple like paper, and the floats rip open like biscuit tins. At sea (at the time of which I am writing) a seaplane was about as seaworthy as a canoe. (Chichester, *The Lonely Sea and the Sky*.)

After my final lesson and rating check, I hosed down the Aeronca with fresh water for the last time, and then drove back to my house on the Eastern Shore. From Back River to the Bay Bridge at Annapolis takes ten minutes in a slow plane, but sixty to ninety minutes by car, in amongst ten thousand other cars crawling along the road like so many cockroaches. I thought about the directness of flying, and I thought about the view I was missing from the ground, that from only four hundred feet above road level, the field of vision would be a hundred times enlarged. Still preoccupied with the pleasures of flying, I drove across the Bay Bridge and looked without enthusiasm at the boats, which on the Chesapeake are all too often—if they have any sort of keel—confined to narrow, buoyed channels and lack the freedom of airplanes to take any path their pilots choose.

Early in the spring of 1989, I began looking for a seaplane to buy. Two or three dozen used seaplanes were listed for sale in *Trade-A-Plane,* the yellow aviation trade paper that covers the whole country. I pursued these leads, telephoning New York, Florida, Massachusetts, Maine, Minnesota, and Tennessee. There was a likely-looking Cessna for sale in Maine, a Type 172, with a low-time engine. But the owner had sold the floats separately before I called him. And "Greg," in Minnesota, had changed his mind about selling his plane: ". . . the float package is too hard to come by. But I know a guy who might sell. . ."

The last ad was for a Cessna, Type 140, with a 135 h.p. engine and extra fuel tanks. I went to Chattanooga to see this plane, and it looked very clean, so I bought it. It was mounted on two EDO aluminum floats, each about fourteen feet long, with a "step" on the keel about halfway back to break the suction on take-off.

The fuselage was of aluminum, too, but the wings were fabric covered, which is not only lighter than metal but perhaps safer since periodic replacement of the fabric will show up any corrosion of the aluminum wing spars. Best of all, this particular airplane carried fifty gallons of gas in four wing tanks and had a range in still air of 575 miles. Almost as important, the engine was equipped with a self-starter.

Manufactured in 1946, it was an airplane that could have belonged to an earlier era, 1925 maybe, when the EDO Corporation of College Point, New York, introduced the aluminum float. (Its top speed, 100 m.p.h., had been surpassed in 1912 when a French-built Deperdussin monoplane won the Chicago Air Races at a speed of 108 m.p.h.) Like most light aircraft of her time, the Cessna 140 was powered by an air-cooled engine, an altogether simpler and lighter power package than an automobile's, having neither radiator, flywheel, nor gear train. This particular plane, an early production model, had been re-engined twice: first to replace the original 85 h.p. engine with a 100 h.p. engine, and then—much later, after it was converted to a seaplane and needed more power to get off the water with the 135 h.p. Lycoming, another air-cooled four-cylinder engine, with a displacement of 290 cubic inches instead of 200 c.i.

When I bought it, the plane was based on Lake Chickamauga, near Chattanooga. It was a long way back to Baltimore, more than a day's flying, I figured, because I would have to go round the bottom of the Appalachian range rather than fly directly across the mountains, whose tops were likely to be in clouds. I could expect to get to Norfolk by the end of the first day, but that would require refuelling halfway. I could land at any one of the boat marinas along the way, but they would be congested because of the Memorial Day holiday. And I did not relish the prospect of a collision with a boat or jetty—or any contact with boaters unfamiliar with the particular vulnerabilities of seaplanes.

Only one suitable landing place on my route was listed in the seaplane directory. That was at the Piedmont Bible College, in Mocksville, North Carolina. I telephoned them and they said, "Come on in"; then, by way of apology or explanation, "It's only a pond."

My newly-acquired airplane had no radio or radio-navigational aids, only a magnetic compass. I took off from Lake Chickamauga in hazy weather and headed southeast, to go around the bottom of the Appalachians before turning northeast to my destination. The compass spun erratically in its housing. Later, someone noticed that there was no kerosene in the housing to dampen the vibration.

The tops of the mountains were in clouds, and I flew alongside the foothills as a seaman follows a strange coast. I went around the bottom of the mountain chain, and flew alongside the east ridge. I didn't know where I was. I was headed over country I'd never travelled, towards landing areas I didn't know, in a machine on which I could barely claim competency. It was a delicious feeling of uncertainty.

After fifty minutes I flew past a water tower with a name painted on the side: "TOCCOA, GA," a town just over the Georgia border from South Carolina. As I flew on northeast, the sky gradually cleared. I flew low over Greensboro, North Carolina, looked down on the city and at the lines streaming back from the bow cleats on the airplane's floats.

I found the pond at the Bible College without too much trouble (there is an adjoining airstrip clearly visible from the air), and I circled over it and saw a man and a boy fishing off a pier. I buzzed the airstrip to let the aviation personnel know I had arrived (it was a holiday, after all), and splashed down onto the pond doing "ducks and drakes," like a flat stone skipping across the water. A man who turned out to be the chief instructor came down to the pond and directed me to a beach. There he refuelled my seaplane from a gas truck and pumped water out of the floats.

In the flight office, I looked at the wall maps of Brazil, where the school sends a quota of missionaries after the chief instructor has taught them to fly. That was his purpose. What was mine? he asked me.

"To fly to the Pacific," I told him.

"I flew a Super Cub all the way from Alaska," he said, "but it flipped over on this lake during a training flight. It's in the hangar there, wrecked." (I took this to be an encouraging thought, that if a plane can crash with a chief instructor aboard, then there's no shame in a novice having a crackup or two.)

Ready for take-off. The "pond" was smaller than the extensive stretches of water at Back River and Lake Chickamauga; besides, the plane was fitted with a fixed-pitch "cruise" prop, which favored cruise flight at the expense of take-off and climb. Nor was there any head wind to help shorten the take-off run.

I taxied right to the edge of the water, lowered the flaps twenty degrees, and raised the water rudder. I looked back at the Bible College, and then to the heavens for any sign of wind. Within seconds a head wind came up and rippled the water. Now or never: I opened the throttle, plowed across the pond, and got the plane onto the "step." As the far shore came up, I tugged back on the yoke to pull the plane off the water, but this action submerged the rear ends of the floats and slowed me down. I tried again. Same result. To the watchers on the shore—the chief instructor, the man and the boy fishing off the pier—the take-off must have resembled that of a cormorant, when its webbed feet drag the water in a series of splashes.

Finally, I succeeded in pulling the seaplane off the water and over the dam at the end of the lake, barely clearing the trees. When I saw that I had done this, I felt that I could do anything. I flew off into the clear blue sky towards the northeast, singing.

Most of the time I was only a foot or two above the water. . . . The exhilaration of the flying stimulated and excited me til I felt half intoxicated with it. It was an almost incredible delight that I had never been introduced to before, and it left the once considered marvel of landplane flying as a dull old show. (Chichester, *Ride on the Wind*.)

After an hour, I passed another watertower, "HENDERSON, N.C." This was good progress. Why not skip Norfolk and its unknown landing area at Chesapeake and go on to Baltimore? Why not? I was not under "air traffic control." I was free as a bird. All I needed to do was find my pencil and draw a thick black line on the chart direct to Baltimore, then alter heading to fly along that line.

Soon I saw the office towers of Richmond miles ahead on the horizon. Then I passed low over the seven rivers—the James, York, Rappahannock, Potomac, Patuxent, Severn, Patapsco—that flow into the Chesapeake, and finally arrived over Back River, the surface of which was chopped up by the wind. I buzzed the adjoining air strip and caught Mike Forster, whom I had not given advance notice of my arrival, just as he was leaving for home. He came down to the beach with his helpers, and they pulled the plane out of the water. This, an eight-hour trip, was my first solo flight in a seaplane.

Which Way to the Coast?

In July 1793, Alexander Mackenzie became the first man to cross continental North America, a forty-five hundred mile canoe trip to the sea, the culmination of three hundred years of American exploration that had begun with Christopher Columbus in 1492.

*F*inding a way across the North American continent involved two prior steps: the adoption of the Indian canoe, and a solution to the geographical puzzle of the North American waterways.

The first European to appreciate, and to appropriate, the canoe was Samuel de Champlain, Commandant of New France. Intent on crossing to the Pacific (he had once seen that ocean from the Isthmus of Panama), he sent three of his followers up the St. Lawrence River from Mont Royal in 1611. Their French-built longboat capsized, and two men drowned in the Lachine Rapids. Soon after, Champlain himself ran the rapids. He did it the Indian way, as a passenger in one of their canoes. "With the canoes of the savages one may travel freely and quickly across the country," he reported. By 1615, he had reached Lake Huron by canoe, pioneering the route of the voyageurs, the French-Canadian fur traders.

Champlain's successors eventually came up with two possibilities for crossing the continent: either follow the Missouri, whose mouth had been discovered by Marquette and Jolliet in 1671, or go west along the Saskatchewan. By 1740, Pierre de la Verendrye, who had established fur trading posts from Rainy Lake to Lake Winnipeg, had selected the Saskatchewan. Then he died.

The English, meanwhile, placed their bets on a Northwest Passage *around* North America. Commencing with Sir Martin Frobisher's voyage in 1576, this venture (". . . the only thing in the world left undone wherebye a notable mind might be made famous and fortunate," said Frobisher) was climaxed by the loss of Sir John Franklin and his party in 1847, halfway along Canada's Arctic coast.

Fifty years before Franklin disappeared, a methodical Scots fur trader had, more or less in his spare time, used the techniques of the French and the Indians to cross the continent. Alexander Mackenzie, a twenty-nine year old fur trader of enormous energy and keen intelligence, used French-speaking voyageurs, with Indian guides and an Indian-designed canoe, to reach the Pacific.

Mackenzie's route followed a complex of waterways that took me some time to unravel. Nor was the problem immediately resolved when, sometime in 1989, about the same time I acquired my seaplane, I got the stack of detailed aeronautical charts from Ottawa. These charts, placed side by side—a great expanse of green, brown and blue—covered the floor of my living room. As I studied these charts, the encyclopedia's confident summary of Mackenzie's trip dissolved into watery details of what seemed to be millions of lakes and hundreds of rivers. What I didn't have was a detailed description of Mackenzie's route.

When I punched the keys on the computer in the county library, searching under "author" and "subject," I drew a blank on Mackenzie, Alexander. Had he slipped through the cracks of history? Could the librarian help? He delved into a fat reference work and announced that Mackenzie's book, first published in 1801, had been reprinted in the American Explorers Series: *Voyages from Montreal on the River St. Laurence through the Continent of North America to the Frozen and Pacific Oceans in the Years 1789 and 1793.*

Preparations · 17

By studying Mackenzie's *Voyages,* and Eric Morse's *Canoe Routes of the Voyageurs* (1961), I arrived at what I thought was a useable summary of the route taken by Mackenzie, even though Mackenzie's book in its unannotated version is not easy to follow, and Morse does not deal with that part of Mackenzie's journey from Lake Athabasca to the Pacific Ocean. Mackenzie's trans-continental route, I learned, was made up of two parts: (1) the main fur-trade trunk line from Montreal to Fort Chipewyan, on Lake Athabasca, which was developed from 1615 to 1786; and (2) Mackenzie's own discovery, in 1792-3, of a trail from Fort Chipewyan to the Pacific Ocean, by way of the Peace River, and then overland to Bella Coola, in what is now British Columbia.

1. Montreal to Lake Athabasca

The main canoe route of the fur traders, which Mackenzie followed for the first three thousand miles of his journey to Lake Athabasca, was strung together mostly by the French from existing Indian routes. It was a process of trial and error that took over a hundred and fifty years. Today, even with modern maps, it is not at all obvious why the fur-trade trunk route across the intricate Canadian waterways went by way of the Methye Portage and the Churchill River. That the trunk route ran so far north as Fort Chipewyan, on Lake Athabasca, was as much a function of the location of thick-furred beaver as it was of the geography of waterways.

"In the whole 3000 miles of the Voyageurs' Highway between Lachine and Fort Chipewyan," says Eric Morse, "there were about 120 portages, 200 "décharges" [where the unloaded canoe was lined through the water] and over fifty lakes big enough sometimes to halt the fur canoes."

Though this part of the route had been explored before

Mackenzie's time, it remained unsettled except for fur-trading posts. Because it was still more or less unknown to the world at large, Mackenzie described it in considerable detail. Morse, though, provides a more concise summary of the stations along the route and the way the system worked, emphasizing the controlling necessity to squeeze a year's operations into five months.

The basic organization of the Montreal fur trade was to have two sets of canoes (each adapted to its own waters) rendezvous half way, swap loads and return, thus licking the problem of covering a 6,000 mile return trip in the five ice-free months.

The rendezvous point, where furs from the Northwest were exchanged for trade goods from Montreal, was on the northwest shore of Lake Superior, at Grand Portage, later moved to Fort William.

2. Fort Chipewyan to the Pacific Ocean

High on the wish list of the fur traders was finding a navigable route right through to the Pacific, so that they might more easily tap the rich source of furs in the Northwest. They wanted to ship trade goods in by sea *via* the Pacific Coast and ship furs out the same way, thus solving the problem of their overextended transcontinental route from Montreal.

Fort Chipewyan, the most important fur trading post of the Northwest, was also ideally situated as a home base to explore that part of the American continent. Fort Chipewyan has access by water in four directions: to the south, by the Athabasca River; to the north, by the Slave River (and thence the Mackenzie); to the west, by the Peace River; and to the east, at the far end of Lake Athabasca, by the Fond du Lac River.

Mackenzie was stationed at Fort Chipewyan from 1787 to 1794. He had taken over the North West Company's trading post from Peter Pond, who had discovered the Methye Portage over the Arctic watershed in 1778, thereby opening up the Athabasca country to the fur traders. Pond inspired Mackenzie with his maps of the Northwest based on his own travels, researches, and guesses.

In 1789, Mackenzie attempted to reach the Pacific by way of an inland Northwest Passage shown on Pond's map, a fanciful linkage between the Great Slave Lake and Cook Inlet in Alaska. He was disappointed when the river he followed—later named after him—ended in the Arctic Ocean (he called it the "Frozen Ocean"), 1,540 miles from Fort Chipewyan. He named it River Disappointment.

Mackenzie determined to try again to reach the Pacific and three years later he left Fort Chipewyan once more, this time going west up the Peace River. Apparently he hoped to find a broad river avenue to the Pacific, easily reached by portage from the east-flowing Peace River. But taking nothing for granted, and appreciating the great distances and short summer seasons of the Northwest, Mackenzie planned a staging post for his expedition.

The Pacific coast is no farther from Fort Chipewyan than the Arctic coast, as Mackenzie was aware, since he knew the longitude of the Pacific coast. He could, therefore, have attempted to complete the trip in one season. It was the Rocky Mountain barrier that dissuaded him. Because the Peace flowed east, Mackenzie knew he had to cross a divide and find a seaward-flowing river, an extra step unnecessary on his trip to the Arctic. Instead of 102 days away, as on his Arctic trip, he was away eleven months on his trip to the Pacific. The actual net time was 130 days, after allowing for 190 days in winter camp, and sixteen days expended going too far down the Fraser. It was a tougher trip to the Pacific, both because of the terrain and the problem of finding the way.

Mackenzie left Fort Chipewyan on October 10, 1792, intending to go as far west as he could that season before the winter snows. Three weeks later his party reached the confluence of the Peace and the Smoky rivers, and there camped for more than six months, hemmed in by snow and ice. On May 9, 1793, the expedition resumed, setting out in a 25-foot birch-bark canoe, with six voyageurs, a Scots assistant named Alexander Mackay, and two Indians as hunters and interpreters. Because variants of the Algonkian language were spoken by all the Indian tribes from the east Coast to the Rockies, these interpreters could be relied upon as far as that point. Beyond the Rockies, communication would be more difficult.

Mackenzie's party paddled and poled for thirty-five days up the Peace River to its source at the end of the Parsnip. Their Indian guides, whom they had to recruit continually as they progressed into new territory, then took them over to the south-flowing Fraser River. It proved to be impassable. Mackenzie and his party had to retrace their route up the Fraser having lost sixteen days and ask for new directions from Indians they met in those parts. They were told to proceed west, on foot, along a tributary of the Fraser which Mackenzie called the "West-road River."

After seventeen days, they came to Bella Coola, at the head of a fiord on the Pacific Ocean. It was not at all an obvious terminus, but it was the conclusion of the first overland crossing of continental North America.

Distance

The approximate canoe distance from Fort Chipewyan to the Pacific was: 945 miles along the Peace River; 145 miles to the source of its tributary, the Parsnip; 170 miles from the source of the Parsnip, by way of the Fraser, to the mouth of the West Road (Blackwater) River (this does not include Mackenzie's diversion down the Fraser); 220 miles overland to the Bella Coola River; and 35 miles down that river. This total, 1,515 miles, must be added to the 3,000 miles of the Voyageurs' Highway.

Time

 Our time was so precious. (Mackenzie, *Voyages*.)

The fastest canoe from Montreal to the Pacific couldn't complete the distance in one short season. The faster seaplane would also have to time its journey to the season of open water. At the farthest point north on the route, at Fort Chipewyan, the seaplane anchorage at Small Lake has open water only from July to September. If I were to leave, say, June 20 from Montreal, I would have ample time to get to Fort Chipewyan by the beginning of July. And all summer to get back.

Flight Planning

I forgot . . . Atkinson's Epitome of Navigation . . . and send me what Quick Silver you have . . . with the sextant. (*Alexander Mackenzie to Roderic Mackenzie, January 10, 1793*)

The charts I received from Ottawa were designed for contact flying, and prepared to a scale of one to a half-million

(1:500,000). At a cruising speed of ninety-five miles an hour, I would cover about twelve inches over the chart in one hour. The charts' detail would be adequate for my purpose and enable me to follow Mackenzie's route, as he described it, pretty closely. Or so I thought.

Seaplane landing and refuelling points are represented on the aeronautical charts by the symbol of an anchor. Information on these anchorages is contained in the *Canada Water Aerodrome Supplement,* which provides pertinent details on about 450 water aerodromes, including, in many cases, diagrams of the landing areas.

Without this directory, the trip would have been vastly more difficult to plan. Without it, I wouldn't have known where to get fuel and would have been in the situation of the Lindberghs who, in the summer of 1931, flew their seaplane across Canada from New York to China and had to arrange for fuel caches to be laid down ahead of time; or of Francis Chichester on his seaplane flight, that same year, from Australia to Japan:

> I was very soon in difficulties about devising a continuous route. Every five hundred miles at most, I must find a river or inlet sheltered enough for a 1,150 lb seaplane to ride out the night at a mooring, without being swamped by waves or blown on its back by the wind, where someone lived who could understand my talk or signs, and where I could obtain some petrol. (Chichester, *Ride on the Wind.*)

My flight would be duck soup compared to those pioneering flights. All I had to do was to mark Mackenzie's route on my charts and then select convenient alighting points along that route. Because Canada depends so much on seaplane travel, there is a sufficiency of water aerodromes available, even on the prairies of Western Canada. One gap in the chain—a change in fuel availability, for example—could spoil the flight, though. Even with my plane's extra range, I didn't care to plan long flight legs without the alternative, in the event of bad weather, of turning back.

During the winter of 1989 I spent many days poring over the charts and directories, and I listed every water aerodrome on Mackenzie's track. In this way, I arrived at a working list of suitable landing places along the transcontinental canoe route. Within this framework there was scope for flexibility. I would have the option, for example, of overflying Bella Coola with its "unsheltered harbor; fuel in drums," and substituting nearby Bella Bella, sixty-five miles beyond, which has better facilities.

What about navigation? I checked out Chichester for ideas. His flight across the Tasman Sea, in 1931, from Aukland to Sydney, involved several hops between tiny islands and required perfect navigation by sextant—and rebuilding the plane when it capsized at its mooring at Lord Howe Island. This was not what I had in mind at all. I expected to find my way across Canada by looking out of the window. "Pilotage," also known as "contact flying," depends upon reference to visual landmarks. For my route, these would be rivers and the shorelines of lakes.

The only tricky legs I expected—those without good landmarks—were in the lake country of Quetico-Superior and along the Churchill River, and in the mountains of British Columbia. My longest leg without the possibility of refuelling would be 380 miles, along the Peace River, from Fort Vermilion to Fort St. John.

It all seemed so simple: no reconnoitering of rapids or searching for portages, just sail over the top. It was nice to be a fly-boy. (But there was the nagging worry that, once down on the water, I was out of my element.)

Behind the Eight Ball

🙢 . . . a hole was broken in her bottom, which occasioned a considerable delay, as we were destitute of the materials necessary for effectual reparation. (Mackenzie, *Voyages*.)

*B*y waiting until May 30 to acquire a seaplane, I had unintentionally forfeited the summer season of 1989. There was insufficient time, I now realized, to plan the route, check out the plane and practice flying it, and—besides—to deal with matters more or less pressing and unconnected with flying (these included a new interest in a strawberry blonde). Thus, the fitting out of the seaplane for a flight across North America promised to become a leisurely process, undertaken over twelve months time, rather than a helter-skelter process crammed into a few weeks. It didn't quite work out that way.

Item: Slipping & Skidding

My little seaplane was "squirrely" in the air because of a lack of directional stability arising from the relatively large floats. When floats are attached to a landplane, the extra side area of the floats that is ahead of the turning axis of the airplane reduces the effect of the tail. Like an ill-fashioned wind vane, the plane may set crabwise relative to its passage through the air. At slow speeds in this condition, especially in a turn, one wing could lose lift, and the plane would flip over in a stall and spin.

To correct this condition of skidding flight, my plane needed continuous help from the rudder. But which rudder pedal to push I could determine only if I knew the relative wind. My first thought was to attach a tuft of wool to the base of the front windshield with tape, an idea borrowed from glider pilots, who had in turn adapted the "telltale" used on the backstay of a sailboat to see this relative wind. But I feared that spray would loosen any tape applied to the windshield, so I attached an inclinometer, with two machine screws, to the cockpit dash.

This instrument, which has been in use at least since World War One, looks like a carpenter's level. It is a curved glass tube containing kerosene and a steel ball bearing, which is free to move in the tube. Normally, the ball rests at the bottom of the curve, but with any unbalanced forces, such as slip or skid, the ball moves in the direction of that force. The old-timers, who weren't such seat-of-the-pants fliers as they claimed, watched this ball, and kicked in left or right rudder to keep it centered.

Item: Weigh Airplane

In this slender vessel, we shipped provisions, goods for presents, arms, ammunition, and baggage, to the weight of three thousand pounds, and an equipage of ten people. (Mackenzie, *Voyages*)

I, too, expected to carry a heavy load of gear on my trip across North America. And that gear would have to be loaded properly. Flying an airplane with the center of gravity too far aft because of an unbalanced load is, at best, an unpleasant experience. At worst an unbalanced load can result in a tailspin and crash. But where were the plane's weight and balance computations? Gone astray. As soon as I could get around to it, I rented two 1,000 lb. Fairbanks-Morse scales and enlisted Mike Forster and his helpers to manhandle the scales, one under each float. The sum of the two readings was 1,105 lbs.

To determine the center of gravity of my Cessna seaplane, we removed the scales and balanced her on a two-inch pipe, at the point where the plane would teeter either forward or backward like a see-saw.

A bystander interrupted. "They can't build a better plane now than they did in 1946," he said. It was true. My seaplane looked good: all compound curves—a pretty thing, a bathing beauty, an elegant toy.

We measured the distance back from the wing's leading edge to the plane's point of balance, which was 14.7 inches from that datum.

These figures—the airplane's empty weight and the location of its point of balance—I entered in the airplane log. With this information, I would be able to compute how much of my gear could be safely stowed in the baggage compartment behind the seats, and how much would have to come forward to be strapped to the passenger seat beside me.

Item: Watch the Prop

During the process of readying the plane for its continental flight, I made intermittent test hops from Back River. It was after one of these flights that Mike's helper, Scott, almost lost his head.

When I taxied up to the beach, I saw that Scott had backed the trailer into the river and was waiting for me to drive the seaplane onto it, like a ramp. When I was fifteen feet away,

Scott, who was standing on the trailer just above the waterline, turned his back on me to talk to a bystander. I yanked the throttle right back to slow the seaplane but she had way on her, and kept going, propeller whirring, towards Scott on the trailer. I yelled at him; there was no response. The seaplane kept on, propeller whirring. I screamed, "GET OFF THE TRAILER!"

He was absorbed in conversation and couldn't hear me over the engine noise. The seaplane approached the near end of the trailer. Scott's decapitation was imminent. Who would tell his mother?

I cut the ignition. The propeller slowed and stopped. The seaplane, losing way, slewed around into wind and broadsided the tires of the trailer, then drifted away. Scott looked complacently around, waded into the water, took hold of the grab line attached to the bow cleat of the near float, and pulled the plane back to the trailer.

Drained by this experience, I stopped at the first lounge on the way home to top up on a couple of sixty-cent drafts. There were about forty patrons at the bar attended by three television sets and two of what may have been the biggest and homeliest barmaids in America. Not one of the patrons wasted his time watching the TV programs or the barmaids, but busied himself with his friends and his beer. The lone customer who attempted some banter with one of the barmaids—he tried to hurry her along—was ejected.

Item: Get a Radio

One cold, grey day in November, I drove over the Key Bridge in Baltimore to Martin Airport to see about getting a radio installed in my plane. The sky was leaden, and the waters of Baltimore Harbor, a sickly yellow-green-grey color, whipped up to bobbing white horses by the wind. I drove up to the airport and went into the cavernous, well-heated hangars filled with corporate planes whose polished aluminum skins reflected the light from a multitude of overhead neon lamps.

I looked for the radio shop, missed my way, and stopped in a dingy back office, where I encountered an old man with rheumy eyes sitting at a battered sewing machine.

"Before the War," he said, without any prompting, "I was a tailor, and during the war I had sixty-six people working under me—fifty-three women, and thirteen men—doing the upholstery on the bombers. This plant turned out one B-26 every four hours. If Hitler only knew! Twenty-four hours a day, seven days a week—that was the schedule. But people were different then."

He directed me to the radio shop, where I found a half dozen technicians, seemingly without tasks (it was probably their lunch hour). No one could answer my questions, or knew whether they could service a seaplane at Back River. I never did get a radio installed, but later bought a hand-held transceiver instead.

Item: Repair Hole in Float

I went to Back River as often as I could and worked on my list of "items to be done." In the course of this work I suffered through the whole range of body contortions associated with working in the wing roots (where I installed two aerials, one on each wing), in the baggage compartment, under the instrument panel, and inside a float. For there was now a hole in the right float. It happened this way.

There was no resident mechanic at Back River, and I'd had to wait for an itinerant mechanic to perform the required annual inspection. He didn't come as scheduled in December, when the weather was particularly cold. Or the next two months, when—wouldn't you know it?—a strong anticyclone over Greenland blocked our southern airflow from the Gulf of Mexico.

After about three months, the days warmed, the mechanic came, and I was told by telephone, "The annual is now being done, and we'll repair the hole in the float as soon as we can."

"What hole?"

"We pushed the plane onto the trailer and moved it to a spot near the hangar, where the mechanic could work on the plane more easily; but the plane got away from us while we were sliding her off the trailer, and the right float was punctured by the end of a two-inch pipe."

I looked for the sheet-metal worker who had repaired the two other seaplanes based at Back River, but was told, "He's gone a-hog huntin' in Tennessee." No-one else was able or willing to repair the hole, which was inconveniently located against the keel—hard to get at and tricky to repair because a patch would interfere with the longitudinal strengthener which joined the two undersides of the "V"-shaped keel.

The airport cognoscenti recommended that the hole, or rip, be repaired by heliarc. I called the manufacturer, EDO Float Company, on Long Island, New York, and found that heliarcing wouldn't work for that grade of aluminum. A riveted metal patch was needed. As a temporary measure, I put a fiberglass patch over the hole in the float. Then, supposing that I would have to take the plane elsewhere, and fearing that the patch wouldn't hold up to the pounding on take-off, I placed an inflated bladder in the appropriate compartment to keep out water.

Where would I get the repair made? The seaplane bases at Long Island and Philadelphia were closed to me because I did not have a radar transponder installed in my plane. Nor was anyone around Baltimore prepared to come out and install such a device; one radio shop suggested that I remove the wings and truck the plane to their shop.

The alternatives for repairing the float were: (1) the mechanic in Kentucky, who had installed the floats, or (2) a referral from EDO: Steve Kelly's repair shop at East Haddam, a little way up the Connecticut River from its mouth on Long Island Sound.

Going to Kentucky would entail a 590-mile flight across the Appalachian Mountains and a problematic landing on the grass at my destination. East Haddam, however, was in the direction of Canada, and only 365 miles away. It was the obvious choice.

The first of May, 1990, had come and gone. My sick plane remained parked on the grass outside the flight office. Beyond her little patch of shade, the sun breathed life into the pale land, sea gulls followed the plow, and white sails popped out on the Bay. I was eager to be on my way, but much of Canada was still frozen. I wasn't late, yet.

Item: Getting a Ducking

The obvious way to get to the Connecticut River was to fly up the Atlantic Coast over Philadelphia and New York City. But I had to obey the air regulations and stay thirty nautical miles away from both those busy places. During the third week in May a conveniently clear spell of weather arrived. I visited the weather bureau in person so that I could get a more thorough briefing than by telephone. The day after tomorrow would be the best day, they said.

Next day, I drove to Back River, anticipating an entire day to load the plane, fuel her, cut mooring lines to length, and attend to other details. Then the forecast was changed. Today was the best day to go. But Steve Kelly didn't stay late on Thursdays. Now I was in a rush; the day was slipping away. Mike was not here—he'd moved across the Bay. I asked one of the airport helpers to tow my plane down to the river. "That's your second freebee," he said. I was distracted. What were the arrangements for getting to the water? With Mike's departure, they'd been changed, left to this man, who used his own equipment, and who rightly expected me to pay him. After this was settled, he pulled my plane to the water and I took off.

Almost none of my home-made installations worked. At the outset of the flight, at Back River, the emergency locator beacon sent out its distress signal as soon as I armed it, so I shut the thing off. The LORAN, an apparatus that looks like a taximeter, and is supposed to give the plane's position over the ground—I had added it as an afterthought—wouldn't work because its portable aerial snapped. (I wasn't sorry to dump this device. It seemed inappropriate to my expedition.) The indications of the vertical card compass, an "improved" version of the standard magnetic compass, were badly in error; I hadn't been able to adjust the compensating magnets because of the time lost with the float.

None of this mattered. The all-important portable transceiver radio was in working order. In the rush to get off, however, I had forgotten to check the mooring lines attached to the bow cleats. This would be my undoing.

I arrived over Havre de Grace and turned inland from the Chesapeake Bay, up the Susquehanna River, a narrow, deep river spanned at its mouth by four elegant iron bridges. After a few miles, I left the Susquehanna to find the Delaware River. I maintained my direction over the ground by observing the angle of the sun's shadow falling from tall trees along the way. By this method I picked up the Delaware and followed its course as it cut through a high ridge at the Delaware Gap and then turned east, through rough country.

I left the Delaware near Port Jervis and went on east until I came to the Hudson River, which I crossed at right angles, at West Point, New York. The visibility was over fifty miles—I saw the trifling towers of Manhattan on the skyline—and I gloried in spending a day like this, in a way like this.

When I arrived at East Haddam, I saw a minuscule dock on the east bank of the narrow Connecticut River. I didn't like the look of it. I didn't like the wind gusting down the river. I called out my arrival over the radio and was acknowledged, then I landed near the dock and taxied slowly towards it. Docking a seaplane had been demonstrated to me once, in conditions of no wind. But now the wind had picked up and was blowing down the river so that I would have to approach the dock—upwind, into the current—on my right side. But this approach wouldn't work because I was in the left seat and the right seat was piled with gear. No problem, I thought. I would call on the radio and someone would walk over from the office there and help me dock.

But they had stopped answering the radio (nor were they obliged to be on watch—this was not a controlled airport; they were probably busy with other things). I was left to myself.

Instead of docking alongside, I waited until the wind dropped, then nosed directly into the side of the dock at ninety degrees—against the wind and the current. In a flash I switched off the engine, leapt out of the cockpit and onto the float, picked up the mooring line attached to the cleat on the bow of the left float, and prepared to step ashore. But the line wasn't free—it was looped around the rear float strut. I hadn't freed the line before leaving Back River. Just then a gust of wind stirred up little dust devils on the shore and blew the plane away from the dock, back towards a line of pilings.

Boldly I jumped into the water to save the plane—to stop it drifting away. But I went in over my head and could only hang helplessly onto the float spreaders and look back under the tail, waiting a collision with the pilings. It came twenty seconds later, with a crack, as the wing tip struck a glancing blow to a piling and the water rudder was knocked off its hinges by hitting the dock.

I scrambled out onto the dock. I was soaked through, mortified, and angry. People appeared on shore. I yelled for help, and they came over and took care of the plane.

"Where are your mooring lines?" they asked. "Don't you have mooring lines?"

No. Except for the bowlines, I had no mooring lines ready.

Someone lent me a dry pair of trousers, and I huffed around in these oversized jeans until I got a lift to the jet airport at New London. There I was dropped off to buy a ticket home. I waited, bedraggled, in the bar until flight time. I had a shot of whisky and I looked on the good side of things: I had, after all, delivered the plane to the shop.

"I've gone and banged up the plane again," I told the strawberry blonde.

"So you won't be going, after all."

"Oh, yes. They'll fix it in a week or so."

"Oh. . . ."

Some were by no means sorry for our late misfortune, from the hope that it must put a period to our voyage, particularly as we were without a canoe, and all our bullets sunk in the river. (Mackenzie, *Voyages*.)

Item: Accelerated Schedule

Before the float was damaged, I had asked the strawberry blonde, Carolyn by name, to plan on an August 1st wedding, in Manhattan. Now, with the unexpected delay caused by the float, I needed to make my dash to the sea, out and back, in the course of one month.

It was now the third week in June. The ice had melted on the northern lakes. My plane had been repaired and was ready to be picked up.

Carolyn said, "I'm not happy about your trip."

"Well, let's talk about it," I said.

"I'm jealous. You, chasing after Mackenzie. . . ."

"Why? You're not interested in seaplaning."

"I didn't say I wanted to go."

"Well, what are you talking about, then? Do women ever know what they want?" (I was at my most testy.)

"There you go. You've ended all communication. You always do that."

"I have to go on this trip," I said.

"Well, I've got some ideas of my own."

"You mean you won't be here when I get back?"

"I don't know. How long will you be gone?"

"Long enough to make the trip."

"That means you'll stay away for weeks."

[they said] it would require several winters to get to the sea, and that old age would overtake us before the period of our return. (Mackenzie, *Voyages*.)

P · A · R · T II

Mackenzie's Track

Intending to make a speedy passage along Mackenzie's track, I succeeded in crossing North America in thirty days.

N72475 at her mooring on Lac La Ronge, July 11, 1990, Having no keel, the moored floatplane responds immediately to every wind gust.

Days 1–5

Day One

*E*ast Haddam, June 26, 1990. Ready to go! Keyed up to leave for Montreal, to pick up Mackenzie's trail, I stepped up from the float and got into the cockpit. My helpers untied the plane from the dock, and I switched on the starter. The propeller turned once, slowly. Then the battery died.

There was a delay of three hours while a new battery was sent for and put in the plane. This was supposed to solve a starting problem that had developed in Baltimore, but it would cause me trouble later.

When I studied the Montreal chart last week, I couldn't figure out the airspace restrictions depicted for the city. I telephoned air traffic control there and a jesting Frenchman assured me, "We don't understand them either."

Before I left Back River, I solicited advice there, too. A local pilot volunteered: "Yeah. I been to Canada once, north of Montreal. I flew up to see a friend of mine who was a missionary to the Cree Indians. They lived in tipis. I helped myself to some fuel out of a fifty-five gallon drum. But I left the money."

"How long ago was that?" I asked.

"Oh, that was a long time ago."

Every body had plenty of Letters and news from Montreal except myself. (*Alexander Mackenzie to Roderic Mackenzie, July 16, 1790*)

As it turned out, the nearest Customs entry point to Montreal that would accomodate my arrival in a seaplane was at Drummondville, a town about sixty miles northeast of Montreal, on the St. Francis River. That solved the airspace problem, too, for I wouldn't be landing at Montreal.

As soon as the new battery was installed, I telephoned the Customs office in Quebec. "I expect to arrive later, at three o'clock." Then I went to the jetty, untied the seaplane, and taxied out into the Connecticut River.

I had intended to take off down river, away from the bridge. But the wind picked up from the opposite direction, the northwest, so I had to make the long, slow taxi downwind—slowly, and with the plane's nose held high, to avoid spray damage to the propeller. When I thought I'd gone far enough, I retracted the water rudder, spun around into the wind and took off towards the bridge.

The day was sparkling clear. From the Connecticut River I cut across to the Hudson, the wider avenue to the North, and followed it along its remarkable sunken valley, between the Catskills and Adirondacks on my left and the Berkshires and Green Mountains to my right. This valley points straight up-river to Montreal and leads northward into a chain of long lakes culminating in Lake Champlain, whose surface, on this day, was churned to whitecaps by the long uninterrupted course of the wind.

From Lake Champlain, the Richelieu River flows down the other side of the watershed through gentler country. The landscape changes to a pattern of long narrow fields peculiar, in North America, to Quebec and Louisiana. I followed the Richelieu northwards to the St. Lawrence until, on this same plain, Mont Royal came in sight, looking something like a beached whale with lilliputian skyscrapers along its flank.

I found the St. Francis River, then the seaplane base, and circled overhead. No answer to my radio call. There were two small docks. A De Havilland Beaver was at one dock, but the other was vacant. Two figures stood on the dock near the Beaver. I circled again and noted that the wind sock hung limp, indicating that there was no wind. I lowered the flaps, approached to land, and saw I was drifting across the river, so I put one wing down into the wind that wasn't supposed to be there, and landed, with a plop, in the water. There was a wind after all—the plane slewed around into it—but the wind sock still indicated a calm.

The two figures strolled over to the vacant dock. I was grateful to them. I headed towards the end of the dock, but one of the figures motioned me to the side. I cut off the fuel, the engine sputtered to a stop, and a man caught my strut. I switched off the ignition and got out onto the dock. The second figure was a female customs agent.

"I'm very happy to see you," I explained unnecessarily. "Last time I docked without help, I fell in."

She looked sympathetic and doubtful at the same time.

"How long will you be in Canada?"

"Until the end of the month."

"Where will you go in Canada?"

"To the Coast. To British Columbia."

Again, the doubtful look. She handed me an entry permit, *Ce permis est valide jusqu'au July 30, 1990.*

I looked around me and saw that the wind sock had wrapped itself around its pole, and was immobilized.

I called for a cab and left my plane in the water, promising myself I'd pump out the floats every day of the trip. I didn't intend to find my plane sunk at the dock some fine day.

This evening, as I dressed for dinner, I felt happy and relieved. The flight had been perfect and I was here, outside Montreal, ready to pick up Mackenzie's trail. I put on my bush outfit—a Sears work shirt and khaki trousers—and presented myself at the dining room. The hostess seemed to be unsure whether I had come to fix the plumbing or to order dinner, but she gave me the benefit of the doubt and ushered me to a white cloth'd table.

"What would you like to drink?"

"Beer, please."

"No wine?" she said archly. After dinner, I went to my room, turned on the television set, and noted that I could choose from nine French and three English language stations. The main story was about an uprising by Mohawk Indians in Oka, Quebec.

Day Two

June 27, 1990. The weather changed abruptly today. It turned overcast, cool, and rainy. I had hoped to land my seaplane, with panache, in the middle of Montreal, at one of the anchorages shown on the chart, then pick up the trail of Mackenzie and his voyageurs. Now I was forced to change my plans; I arranged to drive into Montreal in a rented car. Once I had the car, though, I wasn't sure where to go in Montreal.

I checked Mackenzie's book.

The necessary number of canoes being purchased . . . and the lakes free of ice, they are then dispatched from La Chine, eight miles above Montreal. (Mackenzie, *Voyages*.)

I'd start by visiting Lachine.

When Jacques Cartier was appointed by the King of France to find a passage to China, he sailed west across the Atlantic, into the Gulf of St. Lawrence, and up this river until, a little beyond the hill he called Mont Royal, his way was barred by formidable rapids. In a separate attempt, another boat from the expedition was lost, and eight men drowned.

Near these rapids, the head of navigation of the St. Lawrence River, Robert La Salle fixed his base of operations. The house was derisively called La Chine, from its owner's preoccupation with finding a way to China. La Salle, a super energetic man, canoed far to the west, but took the same wrong turn as Jolliet, and ended up on the Gulf of Mexico. Hence Louisiana.

The Île de Montreal is about three times the size of Manhattan Island and is similarly connected to the mainland by numerous bridges. To cross over to Lachine, I would use the Pont Mercier. To get there, I drove through the Kahnawake Iroquois Indian Reserve, on the south bank of the St. Lawrence, and got onto the bridge, which was under repair so that traffic moved in fits and starts. It took forty minutes to cross the bridge. So much for panache. I saw little or no white water from my vantage point on the bridge. A heron flapped slowly overhead. I realized that the rapids would best be seen from the air. The great fearsome rapids of former times was now an obscure piece of scenery tucked away in an urban wilderness.

Where would I draw next?

Leaving La Chine, they proceed to St. Ann's, within two miles of the Western extremity of the island of Montreal . . . which may be termed the commencement of the Ottawa River. At the rapid of St. Ann they are obliged to take out part, if not the whole of their lading. It is from this point that the Canadians consider they take their departure, as it possesses the last church on the island, which is dedicated to the tutelar saint of voyages. (Mackenzie, *Voyages.*)

Now I drove down to the end of Montreal Island, to St. Anne de Bellevue. Arriving there, I parked behind a *brasserie,*

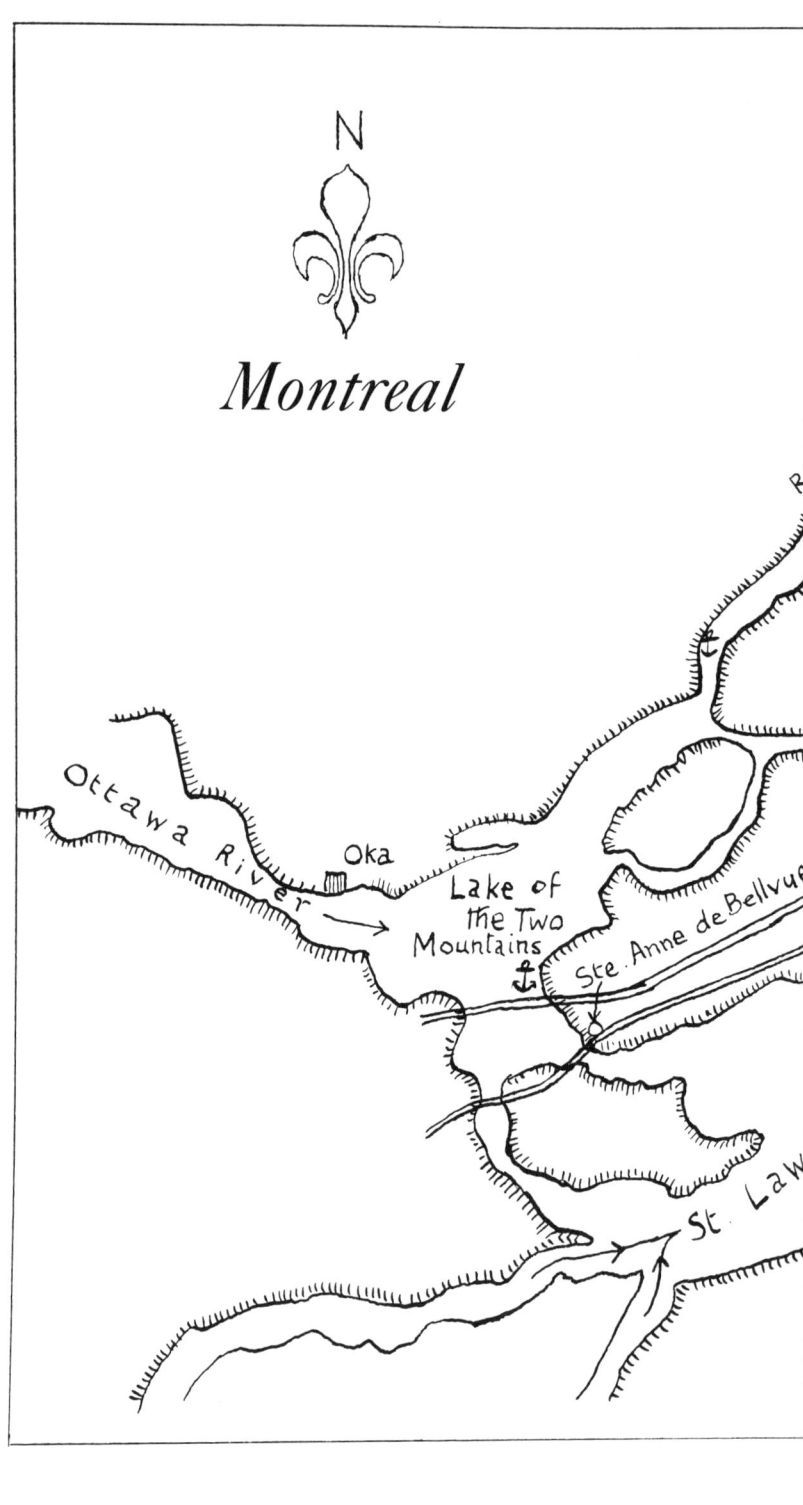

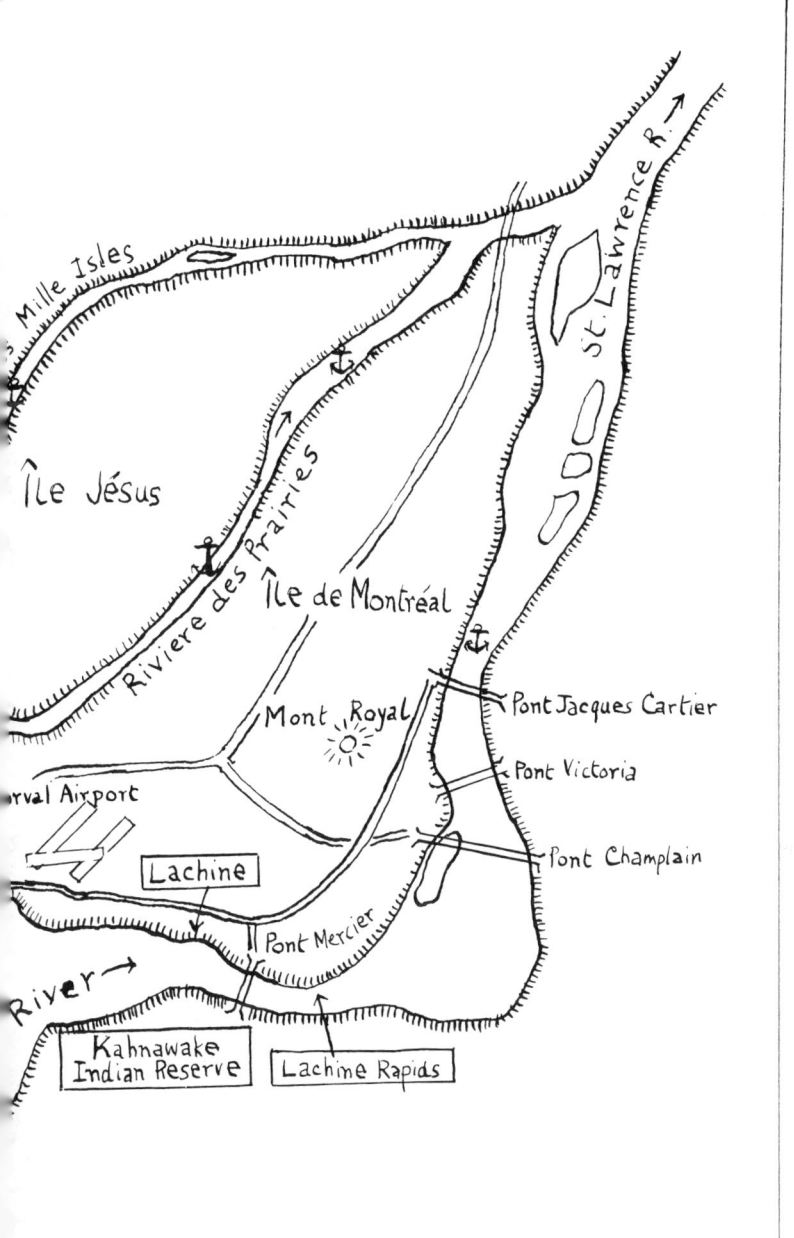

scale approximately 5 st miles = 1 inch

on the bank of the St. Lawrence River, and looked for the church of the voyageurs. I asked a passer-by where it was, but he didn't know. I crossed the road, saw the spire several blocks away, and went towards it, passing a little house whose sign—in English—read, "Simon Fraser lived here."

Here, at any rate, was a trace of one of the Northwesters; on the far side of the continent I would come to a river named after him. But when I arrived at the church, I was disappointed to see that it was not old. I didn't go in. I would cast around afresh.

I returned to the *brasserie* and ordered lunch and a beer and—on inspiration—asked to see a telephone book, as it occurred to me to see if there were descendants—or, at least, people of the same name—of the voyageurs who paddled Mackenzie to the Pacific, and whom Mackenzie names as Joseph Landry, Charles Ducette, Francois Beaulieux, Baptist Bisson, Francois Courtois, and Jaques Beauchamp. This is what I found:

Landry	15½ columns
Ducette	0
Beaulieux	20½
Bisson	5
Courtois	1½
Beauchamp	13

Of the name Ducette, who accompanied Mackenzie on both of his great voyages, to the Frozen and Pacific Oceans, there was no listing. What a shame, that such a famous name should disappear. Still, I might find at least one of these telephone personages who would claim descent from Mackenzie's voyageurs who first made their way overland to the Pacific two hundred years before. I trotted along the street like an impatient bloodhound until I came to a drugstore named Landry. I went in and spoke to the middle-aged man behind the counter.

"Is your name Landry?" He looked at me expectantly, said nothing. "I want to know about your ancestors."

"This is the pharmacy," he said, in awkward English. No, this wasn't going to work.

I got back in my car and whizzed along the limited-access highway, through the rush of traffic in this place of three million people. I glimpsed a roadside sign, brown with white letters, which read *Lieu Historique,* and some other words I couldn't read. This looked promising—a link to Mackenzie's days, when Montreal was a town of ten thousand souls. I got off at the next exit, at Lachine, and went back and found the sign. It read, *Lieu Historique. Le Commerce de Fourrures en Canada.* The Quebeçois do not choose to translate their road signs into English, but it was easy to guess that *fourrures* were furs.

I followed the signs and came to the bank of the St. Lawrence and to a stone building identified as a former North West Company warehouse, now a museum. I went inside and there was a blonde girl lecturing in stilted English to an attentive audience. I was reminded of a toothpaste commercial I had seen long ago, patterned on a French lesson. But she was talking about hats.

"Top hats were worn by men of consequence in Europe. They were made of felt. Felt is made of the downy underhairs of fur-bearing animals. The hairs of the beaver are barbed and cling to each other. They make the best felt. In today's money, such a hat would cost two thousand dollars."

To further titillate the audience, she told them that the voyageurs who transported these pelts in their canoes were so tormented with biting insects that they covered themselves with a mixture of bear grease and skunk oil to ward off the bugs. I hoped these little darlings were low fliers.

After the lecture I went up to her. She said, "I was talking slowly because that audience is trying to learn English."

"What about Mackenzie?" I asked.

"He left from here, from this very spot." Finally he had broken cover. I had picked up the trail.

"I'm going home to Texas," Carolyn said, when I phoned in my position report.

I thought it prudent, however, to take no notice of the transaction, and to wait the issue of future circumstances. (Mackenzie, Voyages.)

Day Three

June 28, 1990. This morning was overcast, gloomy. I went to the dock and took off from the choppy waters of the St. Francis River into a chill northwest wind. Then I flew up the St. Lawrence until I came to the white water of the Lachine Rapids and the old fur warehouse at Lachine. Now I was on Mackenzie's trail, and I intended to keep on it.

By the time I came to the end of Montreal Island, the overcast had cleared, replaced by cloud streets of cumulus. Here I picked up the fork of the Ottawa River, which I would follow for three hundred miles, to its tributary, the Mattawa, and its source at Trout Lake.

The Ottawa flows through pleasant farm lands between Ontario, on one side of the river, and Quebec on the other side, to the north. In the manner of the Rio Grande/Rio Bravo, this river is called the Ottawa on the Ontario side, and the Riviere des Outaquais on the Quebec side. Names mentioned by Mackenzie in his narrative, and which are repeated on the aeronautical chart, include the River Rideau, Fort Coulonge, and Deep River. There are noticeable rapids just above the City of Ottawa and also at Pembroke. But one single image dominated my flight: the Ottawa River flowing from the western horizon, the first of the glorious waterways I would follow across North America.

In Mackenzie's time, the Ottawa valley was part of a huge pine forest that covered what is now southern Ontario, Michigan, Wisconsin and Minnesota. It was a forest that "had no friends whatever because to clear off a few acres of land, they [the settlers] would set fire to miles upon miles of the noblest trees that ever lifted their lofty heads toward the heavens." So said Sir Wifred Laurier, in a speech he made in 1906. An idealist, who was not re-elected Premier of Canada, he no doubt believed that future forest management would be more enlightened.

Beyond Ottawa's copper-roofed parliament buildings, near Deep River, is Pointe au Baptême, where the novice voyageurs were baptised before going into the *pays d'en haut*. Here the country changes abruptly from a pleasant river valley to a wild one. I was flying barely a hundred feet over the cliffs at this point because the terrain had come up on me. I had got out of the cultivated zone. Not so far west as Buffalo, New York, I was in the bush.

When I came to the point where the Ottawa curves off northwest, I left the river to follow its tributary, the Mattawa, a very pretty little river. Then Lake Nipissing came into sight, a big lake, about forty miles long. The seaplane landing area is on the smaller Trout Lake nearby (itself directly on the Voyageurs' Highway), for seaplanes are designed to fly from one sheltered lake to another, not to brave large open areas of water like Lake Nipissing.

I had completed my first seaplane navigation in Canada with ease just by following the chart and by looking out of the window. I'd had no need of compass, or radio aids. Would it be like this all the way?

I saw a dock at the far end of Trout Lake, and I landed and

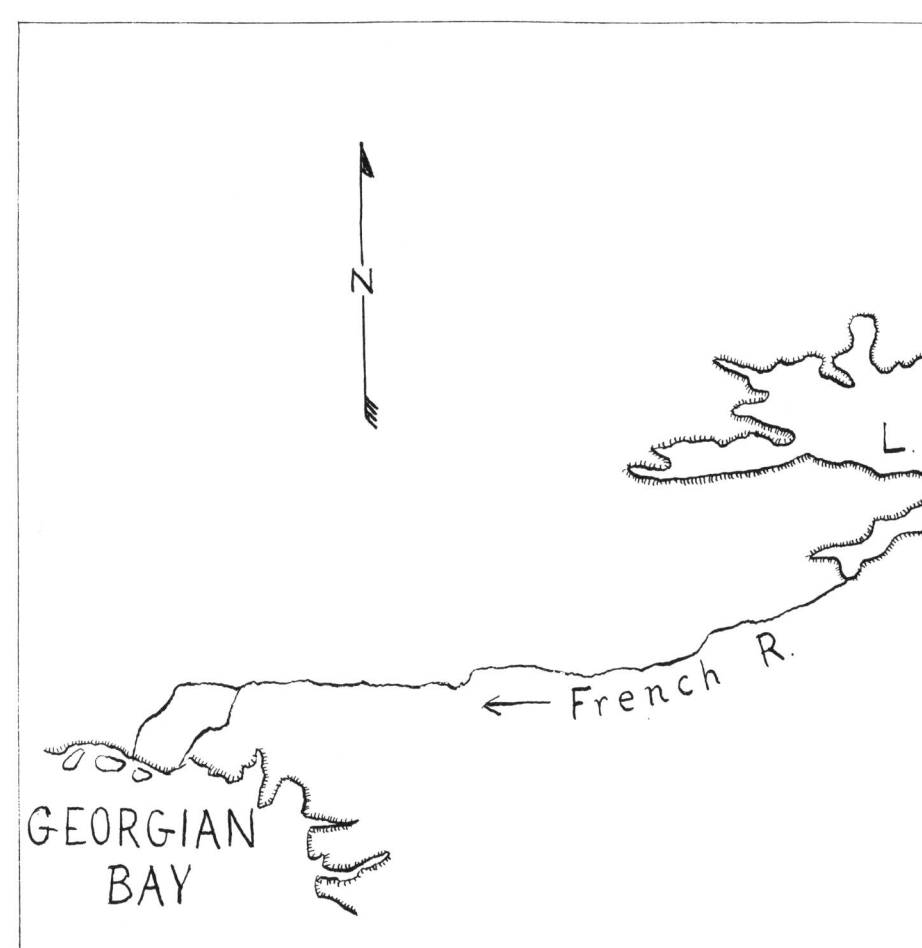

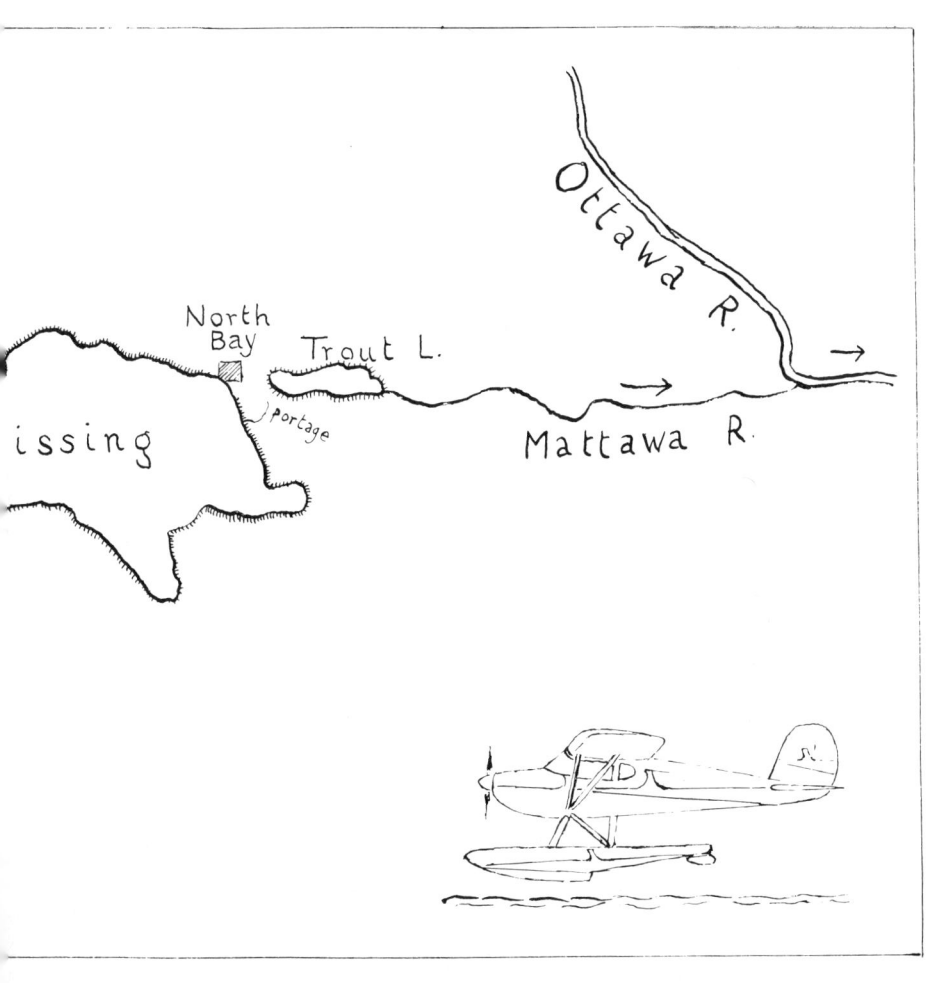

taxied towards it. There was no answer to my radio call. Two men on the dock walked away as I approached. I couldn't dock by myself because of the wind direction relative to the dock, so I taxied past some boaters on the shore and yelled at them, but they ignored me. I taxied in circles, determined to figure something out, and not to be hasty as I had been on the Connecticut River. Belatedly, I was adopting the first rule of seaplaning: "Take your time!"

A seaplane landed near me and tied up to the dock with the help of one of its own crew. I followed and yelled that I, too, wanted to tie up, and the pilot motioned me in and got hold of my strut. He said I couldn't stay there, though, because it was a government dock, and that I should go to the regular seaplane base about a quarter mile along the lake shore. This I did, and I saw about six seaplanes there which I hadn't seen from the air, tucked in against the shore. A man on the dock saw me and helped me tie up. He said he had heard my radio calls, but couldn't reply because the transmitter in the flight office wasn't working on that frequency.

Day Four

June 29, 1990. Grounded by fronts over Manitoba and Ontario. What would I do here? Why, look for signs of Mackenzie.

Here is this small town, North Bay, insignificant from the air, which turns out to be the extensive, still expanding, home to fifty-six thousand people: a place where I am dependent for my transportation on taxis chauffeured by garrulous men who make their business mine—modern-day voyageurs all too ready to tell of their arduous lives.

"I was stressed. I was worn to a frazzle," the taxi driver told me. "I was incontinent. I went to the doctor. 'I can't find nothing,' the doctor said. 'Bring me your work schedule. Ah ha!' he said, 'There's your problem.' "

A second taxi driver, face set in a grimace, desperately navigated a succession of back streets. He allowed himself but one comment. "We're desperate for more traffic lights. Desperate."

And taxi driver number three insisted, "All we got here is snow and ice right through April. Rain ever since. I'm depressed. I can't stand it."

The men . . . went to the Rainy Lake in canoes, laden with packs of fur, which, from the immense length of the voyage . . . is a most severe trial of patience and perseverance: there they do not remain a sufficient time for ordinary repose, when they take a load of goods in exchange, and proceed on their return, in great measure, day and night. Such is the life which these people lead; and is continued with unremitting exertion, till their strength is lost in premature old age. (Mackenzie, *Voyages*.)

Thirsty now, I looked for a drink, and came upon three old lechers sitting on stools, leering at the barmaid, and singing in drunken disunion, "I love her dear-ly . . ."

. . . by four o'clock in the morning . . . we could all give the war whoop as well as Mackenzie . . . , we could all sing admirably, we could all drink like fishes, and we all thought we could dance on the table without disturbing a single decanter, glass or plate. . . . (Reminiscence of the Northwesters, quoted by Campbell, *The Northwest Company*)

Day Five

June 30, 1990. Another rainy day in North Bay. I walked into town and looked into a bookstore which advertised, "100,000

Used Books For Sale," the residue of the townspeoples' reading through many long winters. There was nothing on Mackenzie or the voyageurs. Just how cold is this trail?

Then I saw a business called North West Company, with a sign, "Raw Fur Buyer." I went in. There were Hudson's Bay blankets for sale as well as furs and a display of pelts. These the owner identified for me as a beaver (a brown circle two feet in diameter), a fisher, a wolverine (I didn't know the animal was so large), otters, and white and red foxes.

"They look very pretty," I said. "How is the fur business?"

"Bad. There's no demand. It's the animal-rights activists. One of the two auction houses in town closed yesterday. The other is rocky."

The trail isn't completely cold, then. But nearly so.

It still rained. Lake Nipissing was a very pale brown color, overhung by low grey clouds. I went into an outfitter's to buy a slicker. The shopkeeper looked conspiratorial and announced in a stage whisper, "They're in very short supply. The manufacturers have switched production to condoms. That's where the money is."

I came back to the hotel. From the window of my room there was a view of wet washing hanging on a line. I decided to go over to the seaplane base, pump out the floats, and have the engine oil changed. The mechanic also riveted a paddle holder to the left float, where the paddle would be immediately at hand.

I don't intend to be up a creek without a paddle.

Days 6–9

Day Six

Sunday, July 1, 1990. This morning the sky was crystal clear all the way to the western horizon. A fresh wind carried the sharp smell of pine needles across Trout Lake. I had the feeling, after several days of cloud and rain, that this bright new day was the first day of creation, or a freshly-minted coin, too new to touch.

Once in the air, I reached for my chart—the one I had marked with the course—but I couldn't find it, and I circled Trout Lake groping around for the chart, guessing it had slipped irretrievably under the seat during take-off. Meanwhile, I tried to call in my departure time to the flight service station at North Bay, but there was no answer. What was wrong with the radio? Should I land and telephone them? No. Landing the fully-loaded seaplane, docking it, and taking off again was too much effort just to confirm that flight service had received my call. I searched for and found a one-million scale chart to replace the half-million chart I'd lost.

I glanced out of the windshield and swore. A radio transmitter tower loomed just ahead at my level. Instantly, I banked away from the tower. Then I flew straight and level to get over my scare.

The distance from Trout Lake to Thunder Bay, along the route of Mackenzie and the voyageurs, is 610 air miles, most of which lie along the shores of Lakes Huron and Superior. The most convenient refuelling point is Wa Wa Lake, just inland from the northeast corner of Lake Superior and the old fur-trading post of Michipicoten. But to obtain fuel there, the *Water Aerodrome Supplement* advised that prior notice was to be made to a Sault Ste. Marie air charter company. That company, I found by telephoning, had ceased operations, and their dock had been taken over by local pilot Wayne Roberts. I eventually reached him at his home, and he agreed to sell me some fuel.

I headed west over Lake Nipissing and found the French River. "Scenic rapids," I scribbled, and followed the French downstream to its mouth in Georgian Bay. "Azure, emerald in the shoals, purple cloud shadows," I noted.

The 200 miles from Sault Ste. Marie along Lake Huron's North Channel to the mouth of the French River is extraordinarily beautiful canoeing: hundreds of rocky islets; for miles a 500-foot range of quartz-blanched hills following the coast; and crystal-clear water. The voyageurs on coming out of the French River hugged the mainland, being able for the most part to take advantage of a screen of small islands, often a mile or two deep. If there were a bad wind (the prevailing wind is westerly) they used the screen; otherwise it was faster to stay just outside. (Morse, *Fur Trade Canoe Routes.*)

Today the weather was superb. Fifty such days, spent like this, justify a lifetime. But yesterday, while I was on the ground, poking around North Bay waiting out the bad weather, a small plane crashed here, killing its three occupants.

Little Current, Ontario, July 2, 1990. The bodies of three men on board a single-engine plane which crashed in Lake Huron were found Sunday by divers from the Canadian Forces. The plane was en route to Sault Ste. Marie Saturday, when it plunged into six metres of water in Georgian Bay, about one kilometre from shore at the west end of

Manitoulin Island. The pilot said he was flying into poor weather when he spoke to a marine radio operator at about 9:25 A.M. Saturday. It was the last message received from the aircraft. (*Newspaper Report*)

The last message. Who knows what the last words were?

🛶 Whenever a voyageur met his end on the journey, he was buried on the spot, and a crude cross erected over his grave. The early journals speak of seeing as many as eight or ten crosses clustered together . . . along the lakes, the watersheds, and the rapids. (Morse, *Canoe Routes of the Voyageurs.*)

I arrived over Saulte Ste. Marie at 12:30 P.M., and turned north up the eastern shore of Lake Superior.

🛶 This vast collection of water is often covered with fog. (Mackenzie, *Voyages*)

Fog did indeed lay all along the eastern shore, so I abandoned the course I had plotted along the shore of the lake and followed a power line, a few miles inland, which led up the coast. It was mountainous on this side of the lake—the rim of the Canadian Shield—and there was no place for a forced landing. I and my seaplane are utterly insignificant in this extensive wilderness.

After an hour of flying, zipping along over the trees, I came to the bay where the Michipicoten River flows into Superior, and just inland saw Wa Wa Lake, clear of fog. There below me was a dock with a seaplane. I landed nearby and taxied up to it, but no-one came. There was no wind, so I cut the engine and got out on the left float, and paddled the plane like a canoe to bring the plane gently to the dock. I hopped out onto the dock and caught the strut and tied her up—my first successful unaided docking. I went up to the shack on the dock, but it was locked, although not deserted, for there was a dog tied outside.

I needed to find a telephone to close my flight plan. I had no sooner started to look around when a car drew up. "Do you know where Wayne Roberts is?" I asked.

"He might be in town, in a café. Let's go look for him," the driver said.

We didn't find Roberts in either of the two cafés in town, but after we'd returned to the dock Roberts showed up there. Meanwhile, I'd telephoned the flight service from one of the cafés. I was reprimanded: "You're overdue again."

Roberts let me have some gas, and he did me another favor. He showed me how to file a flight notification instead of a flight plan, because it would allow more leeway for reporting, and the Flight Service System wouldn't get restless if they didn't receive an immediate report of arrival.

I taxied out to take off, and when I let the wind weathercock the plane, I saw that the take-off direction was across the narrow part of the lake, towards the town. I had never really grasped Mike Forster's rule that a seaplane requires twice the take-off distance of a landplane. And I was too green to realize that with so little wind, I could just as soon have taken off down the long part of the lake.

I aborted the first take-off when I could see that I wasn't going to lift off soon enough, and taxied slowly back to the very edge of the lake. The second time, I held the nose high until the front third of the floats lifted out of the water, then I pushed the yoke forward, with much pressure, to force the plane onto the step. The shore was coming up fast. I pulled back on the yoke and the heels of the floats stuck in the water and slowed the plane down. I pushed the yoke forward and picked up speed again. The shore was much nearer when the plane unstuck from the water. I glanced at the air speed indicator. It flickered between forty and fifty m.p.h. I saw the houses and the telephone poles and a garage with a red roof right ahead. For one split second I thought I was going to hit the town, but the engine kept pulling and I skimmed over the garage with the red roof.

Then I headed on around Lake Superior.

Lake Superior is the largest and most magnificent body of fresh water in the world: it is clear and pellucid, of great depth, and abounding in a great variety of fish, which are the most excellent of their kind.

Along its North shore is the safest navigation, as it is a continued mountainous embankment of rock, from three hundred to one thousand five hundred feet in height. There are numerous coves and sandy bays to land, which are frequently sheltered by islands from the swell of the lake. This is particularly the case at the distance of one hundred miles to the Eastward of the Grand Portage, and is called the Pays Plat. (Mackenzie, *Voyages*.)

"Better not fly across the lake in a single-engine airplane," I had been told in North Bay. "If the engine quits, and you have to go down on the water, the swells will roll you over." I didn't take the direct over-water route.

I passed over the seaplane anchorage area at Pays Plat, a place mentioned by Mackenzie. I looked carefully but there was no sign of life. Farther along the shore I came to the Nipigon River and could see Thunder Bay ahead. The seaplane landing area at Thunder Bay is within a breakwater at the north end of the harbor. I took another look at the *Water Aerodrome Supplement,* which I had handy in the cockpit. Under "Remarks," it noted, "Heavy swells. Exposed to S & E winds with heavy seas."

Right now, there was only a light south wind, so there would be no problem. I banked over the seaplane dock. The air was bumpy. The ball skidded off to the right end of the inclinometer. I pushed the right rudder pedal to center the ball, and straighten the plane, then approached low over the shore on a south heading, lined up with the wind and the entrance to the breakwater. Bounce! Bounce! The plane settled on the water and pitched like a see-saw in the swell; when I tried to turn she rolled, and the wing tips alternately dipped near to the water. I yelled something like, "I hate seaplanes!"

I tried to drift backwards to the dock. But with the propeller still turning, the drift did not seem significant, though the little seaplane pitched like a rocking horse in the swell. The swell, I realized, was from *yesterday's* wind. I turned broadside to the swells, gingerly, working the ailerons, and got the plane facing downwind, away from the harbor entrance. The seaplane bucketed along towards the dock. There was no one there. And I knew I couldn't dock the plane myself.

When I got nearer to the shore, I saw a man come out of a shack, motioning me to a ramp. Great! I drove the plane up the ramp and cut the engine.

I got out of the plane.

"You don't mind taking on Lake Superior, do you?" the man said.

"That was as much swell as I want to handle."

"It was as much swell as anyone would want to handle. You could have landed close against the breakwater, away from the entrance."

They have a hydraulic lift here to move a seaplane from the ramp to a parking space, but the narrow floats of my plane didn't fit. As we struggled to pull the seaplane up the ramp, my leg went through a hole in the rotted planking and came out bruised and bloodied.

I had had as many thrills in one day as I wanted to handle: the radio transmitter tower at Trout Lake, the take-off at Wa Wa, the landing at Thunder Bay. I pumped out the floats and took a taxi to town where I checked into this hotel, near the waterfront.

"You want a coffee?"
"No. Give me a whisky."
(Doubtful) "You want C.C.?" (Canadian Club)
(Goes away. Returns; still doubtful) "You want C.C. then?"
"Yes. Do you have soda?"
(Relieved) "You want a coke, eh?"
"Just bring the whisky."
I drank the whisky and contemplated seconds.
"Here's your coffee."

⚓ . . . it is a practice throughout the North-West neither to sell or give any rum . . . during the summer. (Mackenzie, *Voyages*)

The waitresses in this coffee shop, themselves not unpresentable, are yet ugly sisters to a splendidly nubile siren in the scullery. What is the dirty apron, the hair tumbled over her eyes, or the soiled T-shirt, to that arresting figure? She is a voyageur's dream. They never met her like west of Montreal. They made do with the material at hand.

⚓ . . . there were some among my party who observed some hidden charms in these females which rendered them objects of desire, and means were found, I believe, that very soon dissipated their alarms and subdued their coyness. (Mackenzie, *Voyages*.)

✈ *Day Seven*

Thunder Bay, July 2, 1990. To this great entrepôt at Fort William the voyageurs averaged eight weeks from Lachine, paddling up to eighteen hours a day. It has taken me fifteen hours flying. And I am behind schedule already.

But I was bound to take a day off to visit Old Fort William.

Besides, I postphone for a while the unknown hazards of my trip.

Old Fort William is just outside town. I went there in a taxicab driven by a Scotsman, a placid Lowlander, who'd arrived in Thunder Bay thirty years before, and found no reason to move on. He was not someone who would know about Mackenzie, the Highlander.

Modern Ontario is a rich province, and the government has built a sumptuous and accurate replica of the stockaded North West Company post. Fort William was an exceptionally large and well-equipped post. Why not? The trade generated, in Mackenzie's words, "profits surpassing anything in America." The post was named after William McGillivray, who was at various times both a colleague and a rival of Mackenzie. The original fort was located a few miles farther down the Kaministikwia River, where it flows into Lake Superior, and is now built over by a railway yard. It was sited as a result of the Jay Treaty, signed in 1794, which fixed the boundary between the United States and British America, thereby determining which trading posts were on British, and which on American, soil. As a result, the North West Company gave up Grand Portage and relocated the post here, to the "Kam" River; they were also compelled to reopen the old French and Indian canoe route to Rainy Lake.

The voyageurs, as many as twelve hundred of them, according to Mackenzie, spent much of July here. In between carrying ninety-pound packages, two or three at a time, over the portage, they rested, "indulging themselves in the free use of liquor."

The rationale for such a depot was the short season of open water. Time imposed an absolute constraint on the fur traders. The two ends of the Voyageurs' Highway, Lachine and Fort Chipewyan, were each eight weeks from this central depot, that is, a sixteen-week round trip. Because of the early winter, this was barely enough to accomodate the round trip to Fort

Chipewyan from Grand Portage/Fort William. The exchange of goods for the farthest posts was therefore made at Rainy Lake, by a special party from Fort William. This gave the returning canoes a head start on winter.

My visit today paid off because I obtained a Trail Guide to the last leg of Mackenzie's route, from Prince George, B.C. to Bella Coola. The details of this leg have been hazy to me.

Day Eight

Thunder Bay, July 3, 1990. The weather turned bad today. I went over to the seaplane base and pumped out the floats, then walked around town.

Thunder Bay is an assemblage of moderately large buildings with not nearly enough people to justify them. The town reminds me of a little man in an oversized suit. I walked up and down the wide streets without seeing anything or anyone that looked promising. There were some college students with rucksacks; a drunken, panhandling Indian; some old men with fedoras and tired faces. I guessed everyone else was out "doing their thing" in the bush.

In the Grain Bin Bar, there were more old men, lively with liquor.

"I worked for the C.P. Railroad," one of them said.

"No! When?"

"1945 to 1958."

"Stop! You knew Joe Sigaleri!"

"No, I didn't."

"He was a worker! He was tall! He was Italian! Everyone knew him!"

"I didn't know him," said the second man.

"He was the best dynamite man in Canada," said a third. "Before he went back to Italy, he went and smashed that big piano of his. He took an axe and did it. I could have killed him. It was worth ninety dollars to me."

The men left, and the bar was deserted. I picked up a newspaper from the table. It listed all 116 calls received by the Thunder Bay Police Department for, I think, twenty hours, midnight to 8:00 P.M.:

1:03 A.M.	Suspicious auto
1:04 A.M.	Barking dog
1:20 A.M.	Unwanted persons
1:30 A.M.	Elopee.

And so on. . .

Day Nine

Thunder Bay, July 4, 1990. The weather cleared on this third day. I made ready to leave but—when I was pushed off at the dock—the engine wouldn't start. So much for the new battery installed at the beginning of my trip. My helpers had not released their hold on the tail, or the seaplane would have drifted back and fouled the adjoining dock, whose sides were too high to clear the tailplane. (It is possible to "prop" the engine by hand—the "Armstrong Starter" method—but this is no use if, as happened to me now, the pilot must start the engine immediately.)

I laboriously unloaded the airplane at the high-sided gas dock to which the plane was now secured head-on, to protect the tail, so that the mechanic could get at the battery, which was located behind the baggage compartment. Seven loons—I counted them—floated nearby, laughing.

The mechanic decided that a new solenoid was needed, so he and I drove around town in a ponderous old Pontiac searching the auto-parts stores for the part we wanted. When the new solenoid was installed, around 2:00 P.M., I telephoned the weather people and they said the route to Kenora was VFR, that is to say, could be conducted under visual flight rules. "What's the surface wind forecast for there?" I remembered to ask.

"Wind gusting to twenty-five knots."

"I'm not going," I said.

🪶 . . . as the wind did not abate of its violence, we were prevented from proceeding till the morrow. (Mackenzie, *Voyages*.)

I have just read Morse, in his book *Fur Trade Canoe Routes:*

🪶 In the various accounts of travel on Lake Superior, there is a general agreement on the proportion of time a canoe is pinned down by unmanageable wind during the two best months, July and August: it works out to one day in three.

It occurs to me that my schedule doesn't make enough allowance for the wind.

The Canadian Shield

*M*ackenzie's route from Lake Superior to Lake of the Woods coincides with the present border between the United States and Canada, between Minnesota and Ontario. The trail twists through an incoherent assemblage of lakes as it winds through part of the heavily glaciated Canadian Shield—a landscape entirely composed of clouds, trees, and water.

After 1803, a more northerly route was used by the fur-trade canoes from Fort William, joining the former route at Lac La Croix, thirty miles southeast of Rainy Lake. After studying the chart I concluded that I couldn't visually navigate either trail to Rainy Lake—there were no line features to follow.

If I could just get to Rainy Lake, the way from there would be easy: I could follow Rainy River into Lake of the Woods. I fell back upon the earliest of the flier's aids to navigation—the railroad, the iron compass.

Two railroads go west from Thunder Bay. The Canadian Pacific goes to Kenora, where I was headed, but it takes a more northerly track than the waterway that I wanted to follow as closely as I could. I decided to follow the more southerly route of the Canadian National Railway from Thunder Bay to Fort Frances, on Rainy Lake.

Leaving Thunder Bay, I would almost immediately cross the watershed of Lake Superior and pass into the drainage basin of Hudson Bay. This was Rupert's Land, an area of 1,500,000 square miles granted by King Charles II of England, in 1670, to the Hudson's Bay Company, a private stock company headed by his cousin, Prince Rupert of the Rhine.

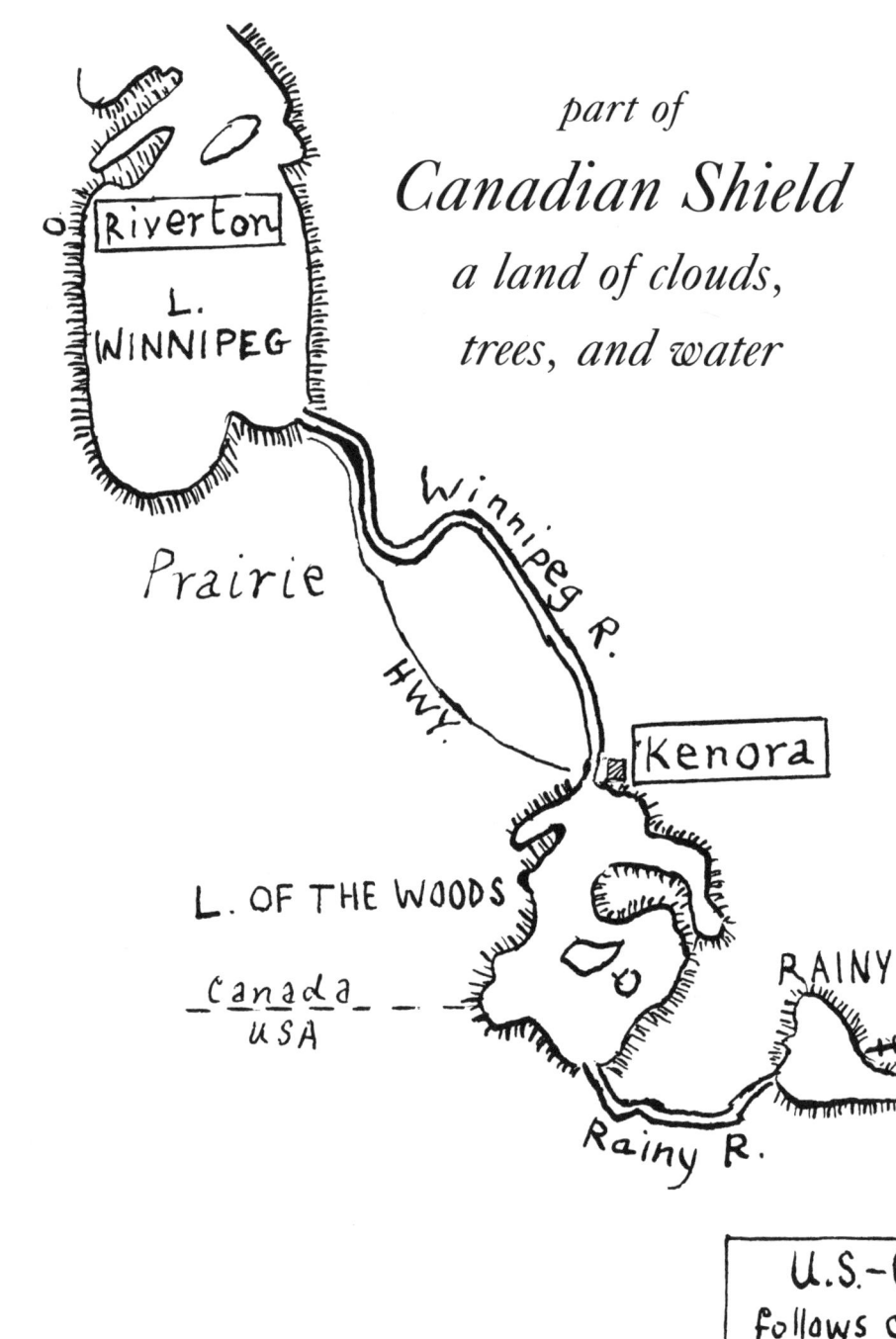

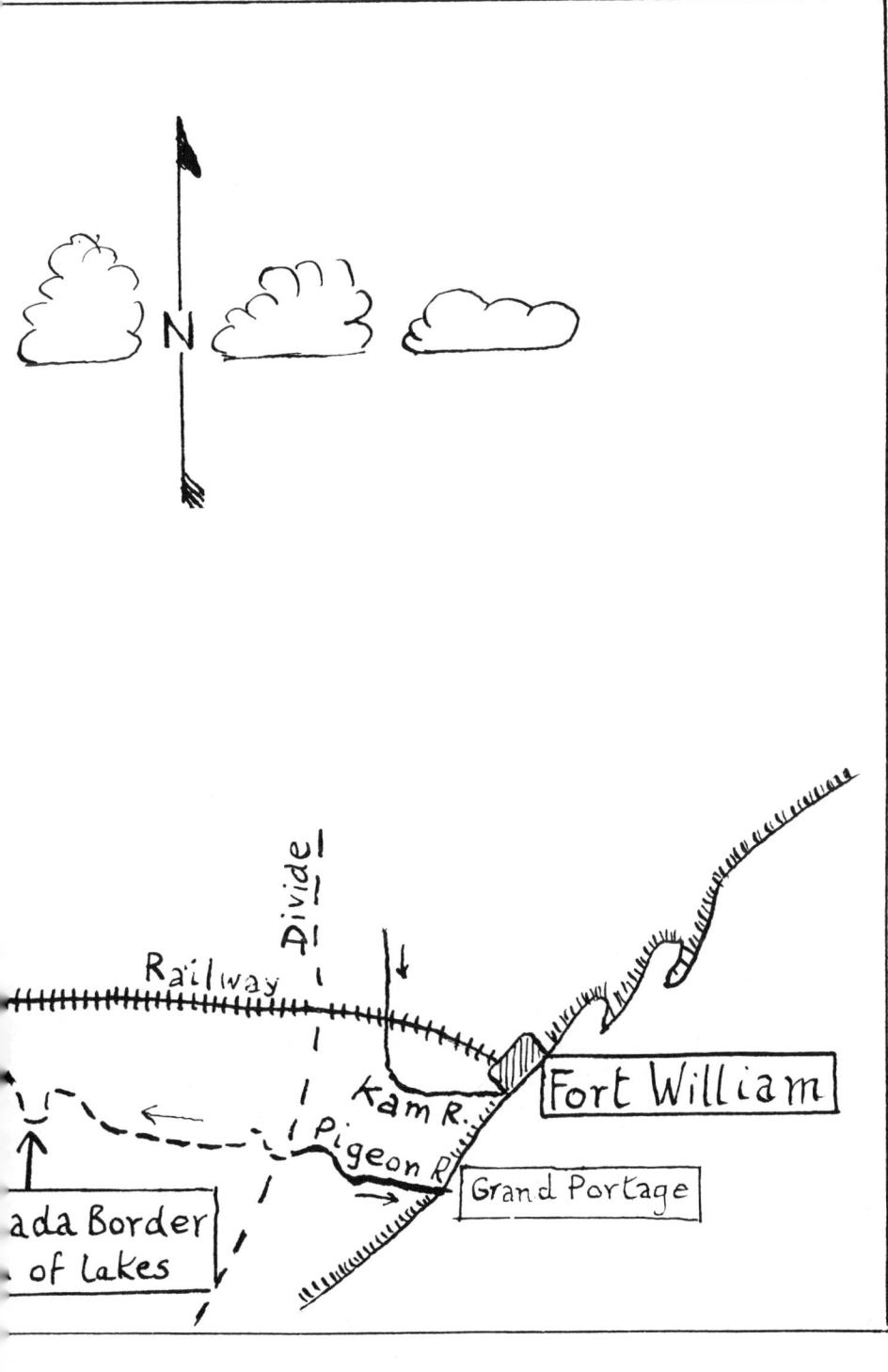

(Rupert's Land does not coincide with, though it overlaps to a great degree, the Canadian Shield.)

Rupert's Land was incorporated into the new Dominion of Canada in 1867, thus linking two coasts under one government. A transcontinental railroad was then planned, patterned after the Union Pacific. Otherwise, the easiest way from Victoria to Ottawa was to take ship to San Francisco, there to entrain for Chicago.

A major engineering problem for the new railroad, the Canadian Pacific, was the building of a roadbed from Lake Superior west across the Canadian Shield to the prairies. Great quantities of fill had to be dumped: one muskeg swamp, a hundred miles west of Fort William, was estimated to be two hundred feet deep.

The route that Mackenzie took to the Pacific is more characteristically North American than any more southerly route could have been. It traversed not only the central plains and the Rockies, but the continent's massive core, the Canadian Shield, "key structure of the continent."

> ... the soul of Canada was to be discovered in the vast stretches of lake, rock, and forest that make up the rugged geography of the Canadian Shield. (Jeremy Adamson, *The Canadian Landscape*)

The Shield is an immense area of ancient rocks centered on Hudson Bay and covering half of Canada. It occurs in the United States in the form of the Adirondack Mountains and the rough country around Lake Superior. These old mountains are part of the initial crust of the earth, eroded over a thousand million years almost to a plain, and subsequently invaded by the ice sheet, which scooped out basins that, when the ice melted, filled with water and became lakes.

The Shield—David Thompson, the explorer, called it the

"Stony-Region"—is a land of rocks, lakes, trees, and swamp. Useless for farming, it is rich in iron, copper, nickel, and gold. Its southern and western rims correspond roughly with Lakes Superior, Winnipeg and Athabasca, and thus with the route of the voyageurs. It is not friendly terrain to pilots.

Perhaps the best-known celebrant of this enormous, distinctive, region is a Minnesotan, Sigurd Olson, who has written of its sights (the aurora, the red maple, the yellow aspen); its sounds (the call of the loon, the howl of the wolf); its smells (the heathers, moss and peat of the muskeg, and the wind blowing over a thousand miles of pine and spruce and balsam); and even the feel of the native stones.

Days 10–12

✈ *Day Ten*

*T*hunder Bay. July 5, 1990. This morning dawned bright, though fog was expected at Fort Frances until 11:00 A.M.

I went to the harbor, sniffed the cool air, and put on my life jacket. I taxied out to the breakwater, faced the plane back to the shore, and took off to the northeast, committing myself once more to the disorganized domains of sky and bush. Once in the air, I searched around a bit, then flew west along the railroad, under a layer of stratocumulus clouds, and over a two-tone forest of dark conifers and light-green deciduous trees.

There was a big hole in the cloud cover over Rainy Lake, allowing the sun to shine through and change the lake's color from gray to blue. From Rainy Lake, which is very irregularly shaped and has many small wooded islands, I came to Rainy River. Now it would be plain sailing.

Rainy River—the name is a corruption of *Riviere de la Reine,* or Queen River—is a generally placid river that flows through fertile farmlands.

> 🛶 This is one of the finest rivers in the North-West. Its banks are covered with a rich soil . . . which, in many parts, are clothed with fine open groves of oak, with the maple, the pine and the cedar. (Mackenzie, *Voyages.*)

From the mouth of the Rainy River, I came out over Lake of the Woods.

Lake of the Woods is about sixty miles long and the same wide, with 14,600 islands, and 25,000 miles of shoreline.

🛶 The Lac du Bois is . . . nearly round, and the canoe course through the centre of it among a cluster of islands, some of which are so extensive that they may be taken for the mainland. (Mackenzie, *Voyages*)

Lake of the Woods is a very obvious feature on the aeronautical chart, with the town of Kenora at its north end. This town is on the site of Rat Portage, to which the voyageurs, who had come up from Rainy River, made their way directly across the lake.

🛶 The carrying-place out of the Lake is . . . named Portage du Rat in latitude 49.37 North, and longitude 94.15 West. It is about fifty paces long. The lake discharges itself [into] the River Winipec. . . (Mackenzie, *Voyages*.)

To get to Kenora, I decided to keep to the east end of the lake, pick up the highway on that side and follow it into town.

I was flying under a gray overcast and through scattered showers, but the visibility was generally good. Keeping my finger on the chart, I followed the shore line north, trying to track my progress over the ground. The irregular shapes of the land forms defeated this effort. There was no sign of Kenora where it should have been. Just clouds, trees and water. Where was Kenora? A vague unease settled on me.

Half an hour (?) later, off on the horizon, twenty miles away, off to the right, I saw a town. I searched the map for some such town and finally concluded it might be Kenora—where it wasn't supposed to be. There was no sun, the sky had completely clouded over, so I didn't have any direction.

The problem was that Lake of the Woods—especially its

northern half—is so broken up with islands that I thought I was at the top of the lake when I was only half way up. Thus, I followed what I thought was the far shore line—but to the west, away from my destination.

> The voyageurs seem to have got lost more often in Lake of the Woods than in all the other miles of their long voyage put together. (Morse, *Fur Trade Canoe Routes*.)

I read this part of Morse's account later, after I got down. Had I been forewarned, would I have done any better?

I landed at Kenora and made the usually futile call on the radio for docking directions. There was an immediate reassuring response. I was told to park behind a twin-engined Beech floatplane at the dock next to the town center. Sure enough, there was a man to help me tie up—just as well because I came in at too sharp an angle, cut the throttle too late, and bounced off the dock.

I walked across the road with my bags, checked into this hotel, and sat down to lunch. This is a resort town, a type of place popular in Mackenzie's day when there were spas all over Europe. But Lake of the Woods? It was on the edge of the known world.

"I shoot thirty or forty dogs a year around my place," announced a man near me, complacently. "Keeps 'em away from the chickens."

"I'm just waiting for the right guy to come along," said his companion, looking fondly at the shooter.

"I had to buy my wife a new washing machine," said the man sitting across the aisle, loudly.

"My daughter just bought a microwave," said his buddy.

"My daughter had someone give her a VCR," countered the first.

"I'm gonna get a car phone," said the second man, raising the stakes.

"I'm gonna get an Apple computer."

"What I was goin' to say is: when I was in Houston, I had me a ride on a mechanical horse."

The articles necessary for this trade, are coarse woolen cloths of different kinds; milled blankets of different sizes; arms and ammunition; twist and carrot tobacco; Manchester goods; linens, and coarse sheetings; thread, lines, and twine; common hardware; cutlery and ironmongery of several descriptions; kettles of brass and copper, and sheet-iron; silk and cotton handkerchiefs, hats, shoes, and hose; calicoes and printed cottons, etc., etc., etc. (Mackenzie, *Voyages*.)

Day Eleven

July 6, 1990. A clear blue sky. The forecast for The Pas: "Scattered clouds at five thousand feet, light rain showers, surface wind 190 degrees at seven knots."

I left Kenora behind with whatever clues to Mackenzie it might harbor—not many: Rat Portage was just a neck of land "about fifty paces across," one more place to hurry over.

From Lake of the Woods, Mackenzie took the Voyageurs' Highway down the Winnipeg River to the south end of Lake Winnipeg; then up the lake to its north end and thence by way of the Saskatchewan River to Cumberland House, a major stop-over in those days, just west of The Pas.

As the crow flies, it is five hundred miles to The Pas. I proposed to refuel en route, near the mouth of the Winnipeg River, another traditional stopping place, a reprovisioning place, for the voyageurs. But the dispatcher advised, "Better stop at Riverton, on the Icelandic River."

The course of the Winnipeg River from Lake of the Woods is not in the least easy to follow from the air as it winds through the wilderness of lakes on the southern edge of the Canadian Shield.

> In short, the country is so broken by lakes and rivers, that people may find their way in canoes in any direction they please. (Mackenzie, *Voyages*.)

I thought it would be easier to intercept the Winnipeg River at the point where it leaves the lake country of the Canadian Shield and enters the prairies of Manitoba. To get to that point, I followed Highway Seventeen west from Kenora. After fifty miles, I became impatient to regain the trail—the river—and I left the main road at Brereton Lake and followed a minor road north. After less than ten minutes over the Shield, I realized (from the direction of the sun) that I was flying east.

Just then, the road petered out and I knew I must have taken the wrong fork, a mistake easily made when flying without reference to compass over featureless forest lands. I turned west by the sun. There was a convenient aiming point on the horizon—a big white building that looked like a grain elevator?—thirty miles ahead, and I flew towards it.

In fifteen minutes, I came to the Winnipeg River where it flows west onto the prairies, and then I came to the big white building, which turned out to be the turbine house of a dam, the Canadian version of the Great Pyramid. Six great dams on this river have all but eliminated the many rapids and falls of Mackenzie's day.

Ahead, I could see Lake Winnipeg. I was beginning to feel a long way from Montreal.

> This [Lake Winnipeg] can only be the Japan Sea. (Claude Dablon, Jesuit Explorer, about 1670)

The brightness had faded from the western sky. Over Lake Winnipeg, the sky became leaden. The brown water was whipped to whitecaps in the middle of the lake by a southerly wind—the anticlockwise air flow around an approaching low pressure system.

No canoe course lay across Lake Winnipeg—in any direction. This is probably the worst lake in Canada for small craft. Apart from its dimensions (280 miles long, with a maximum width of 65 miles), it is in the belt of strong prairie winds, and is incredibly shallow—only ten or twelve feet for much of its surface, with an average depth of perhaps no more than thirty or forty feet. The shallowness makes for steep-fronted, choppy waves, not the long swells of Lake Superior. (Morse, *Fur Trade Canoe Routes*.)

I took the shortest route across the Lake, due west, and then turned north along its shore to Riverton. Here, the narrow Icelandic River empties into Lake Winnipeg. The river looked pretty small and I briefly toyed with the idea of overflying this gas stop and going on to The Pas. But the western horizon was now dark, belying the favorable forecast, so I decided to land.

I circled the dock twice. There was no sign of life, so I buzzed the town a couple of times, then landed on the river. Despite its tiny size, Riverton turned out to be a major seaplane base, with a dockful of floatplanes. Still, there was no answer on the radio, and I taxied in circles on the little river until a man appeared at the dock and made room for me by untying one of the seaplanes and moving it forward. The man turned out to be the pilot of a De Havilland Otter based here. An hour after I had tied up, it started to rain.

Riverton is located just below the narrowest part of Lake Winnipeg, where the voyageurs crossed to the western shore, and it is just north of the "sparsely settled line," a line on the map, a frontier in fact and by decree, north of which airmen are required to carry survival equipment.

There is some farming and fishing here in Riverton and, of course, the aviation business, which depends on government contracts to service the outlying Indian reservations, on fire-patrol contracts, and on trips to outlying lakes for sportsmen from Winnipeg, eighty miles by road to the south.

The rain stopped this evening, and the wind became strong and gusty. From my window in the motel, I could see Canada's maple-leaf flag extended from its staff. I wanted a weather forecast, but the television set in my room was remotely operated from the front office ("You can't have controls in the room or the natives will wreck 'em."), and the set wasn't working anyway.

About seven o'clock, I started on a "pub crawl," conducted by the pilot who flies the Otter. There were three stops, the first being the licensed beverage room annexed to my motel. The other two were downtown, a few hundred yards away and, this being North America, a short ride by pickup truck. There was loud music and a lot of young people—where were they all from?—dressed, even in this one-horse town, in the exactly casual "mod" attire of the moment. For the older set—twenty-five and above—hats were *de rigueur,* baseball caps, never to be taken off during waking hours.

One of the party, unsteady on his feet, announced that I was lost. He could think of no other explanation for someone to be flying around by himself, apparently aimlessly, and asking all sorts of questions.

"Maybe he's looking for something?" said a wit.

"Maybe he's looking for stories?" said another. (They were talking across me.)

The Otter pilot perked up. "A month sitting on the dock at Little Grand Rapids will give anyone a year of stories," he said.

"About what?" I asked.
"Indians," he said enigmatically.

Before I left the bar, I telephoned in my report to Carolyn.

As we had almost expended the contents of a rum-keg, I amused myself with the experience of enclosing a letter in it, and dispatching it down the stream to take its fate. (Mackenzie, *Voyages*)

Day Twelve

Saturday, July 7, 1990. Grounded by bad weather. About 9:00 A.M. this morning I went down to the dock to pump out the floats. The Otter pilot was there, just returned from a flight to a far lake to pick up a party of fishermen.

"The weather was bad," he said. "I couldn't see forward so I looked out of the side, straight down."

"Why take a job like that?" I asked.

"You're on your own"; he said, "not just following someone else's rules."

There was a carnival in town, consisting of half a dozen rides, some side shows, and a nail-pounding contest. A man had brought his four dogs to town and tied them to his pickup truck "to get them used to people."

After I had viewed these attractions, I walked over to the library and asked to see the *Canada Yearbook,* to look up the facts on this place. The librarian found me the 1975 edition. "The bigger branches get the new ones first," she said.

Walking back to the motel, I saw a white pelican with black wingtips on the Icelandic River. These large birds, which have a wingspread of nine feet, winter on the Texas coast.

Days 13–16

✈ Day Thirteen

Sunday, July 8, 1990. Sky clear. Forecast for my route on to The Pas: "altocumulus castellanus and isolated towering cumulonimbus."

I went to the dock. No-one was there except another transient pilot who needed fuel. The pilot telephoned someone—the dispatcher?

"You'll have to get Faren," said the voice on the other end of the line. (So I was told later.)

"Is that his last name?" asked the transient pilot.

"I don't know his last name," said the voice.

The transient pilot advised, "Avoid Fort McMurray."

"Why?" I asked.

"Because you have to come in over a steep cliff and land near sand bars."

I made a note of this for the future.

After a while, Faren and the Otter pilot came. I said goodbye to my friends and prepared to take off. The Otter pilot climbed onto the roof of the flight office to see me leave.

Luckily for me, the wind was right down the river. But it was not a slick take-off. First, I taxied across to the other side of the little river so that I could see around the bend. Then, I started the take-off run. But still unsure of the river bank—I needed to take another look for the bend in the river—I interrupted my run to abruptly throttle back and clumsily lower the nose so that I could see ahead.

After I was off the water at Riverton, I took advantage of the section lines beneath me to check out my two compasses. Here on the prairie the roads are laid out on a grid pattern, oriented to the cardinal points and enclosing sections of land each one square mile in area. This is the very northernmost extent of the prairies that stretch down to Texas and, at the time of Columbus, covered the middle third of the continent.

It was an empty ceremony. I was not prepared to make the leap of faith required to follow the magnetic needle and to abandon the sculpted images of river and mountain. The compass could not protect me against the shifting wind, I reasoned.

But I would go through the motions of swinging the compass. My two compasses were a vertical card compass and a conventional magnetic compass, sometimes called a whisky compass because it uses kerosene as a dampening medium to float the needle. I flew short stretches of road on each of the cardinal points, and I wrote down the results. After allowing for the earth's magnetic variation, errors averaged twenty-nine degrees for the vertical card compass and a mere seventeen degrees for the whisky compass. I didn't attempt to correct the compasses because I didn't intend to use them.

The distance from Riverton to The Pas is 330 miles by way of Grand Rapids (the old portage between Lake Winnipeg and Cedar Lake), then along the south end of Cedar Lake and then north to The Pas.

The landscape is flat, featureless, ninety percent coniferous forest, with open glades of light green muskeg, and scattered lakes.

This is the boreal forest, a wide belt of conifers which stretches three thousand miles or so across Canada, bounded by the tundra to the north and a band of mixed forest along its southern edge. This extensive area more or less corresponds to the Canadian "bush."

The town of The Pas is located on the banks of the Saskatchewan River, but the seaplane base is situated at the more suitable Grace Lake, a half mile south of the river and three miles east of town. When I arrived over Grace Lake at 1:00 P.M., rain showers lay to the west of town, and a stiff breeze sent parallel white wind lines across the lake. I saw two seaplane docks from the air but no sign of people. I had called the operator a couple of days before. "Go to the dock beside the house," he had said.

I landed dead into the wind and taxied up to the dock, but there was no-one there. No answer on the radio, either. I couldn't dock the plane by myself because the wind was blowing off the dock, which—to complicate matters—was too tall to clear my tailplane. I taxied to a second dock. It seemed deserted, but then I saw a man in a red jacket. I got his attention and pointed to the dock, indicating that I wanted to tie up. It wasn't at all obvious to me where I should go, and he guided me by hand signals into a shallow basin, covered with algae.

The wind made steering difficult. The plane wouldn't move across wind; it wanted to weathercock into the wind. I tried to beach the plane but cut the power too soon and she drifted back, downwind. I threw a line ashore, twice, to the man in red. Both times it fell short.

There was a lull in the wind. With the door open to catch what wind there was, I tried to sail the plane backwards, to the far side of the little basin where I saw there was space for an airplane. The wind fell calm. I paddled the plane backwards. Just then the wind sprang up and the rain pelted down. The plane picked up speed and drifted backwards towards a docked Cessna 185. "Start her up!" yelled Red Jacket. I turned the ignition key. Nothing! That damned engine wouldn't start again.

The wind kept pushing the seaplane backwards. I tried to guide it with the air rudder. I shouted to Red Jacket to get onto the Cessna 185 and fend my plane off from certain disaster. He rushed around the dock and scrambled onto the front right float of the 185 just in time to fend off my plane, while I danced ineffectually on my left float. The left wing of my plane passed under the right wing of the 185.

When he had secured my plane to the dock, Red Jacket introduced himself: his name was Bruce Pelechaty; he was a fire warden.

"I would have jumped in if it would have helped," he said cheerfully.

"How deep is it?" I asked.

"Not very deep, but there's two feet of loon s--- on the bottom."

Day Fourteen

July 9, 1990. The Pas—nothing remains of its founding in 1750 as Fort Paskoyac—is a raw, utilitarian town on the edge of the Canadian Shield, on the railway line to Churchill. It is a town of ugly 1950's-era buildings on the banks of the fast-flowing Saskatchewan River. Looks can be deceiving, though; the inhabitants wouldn't swap The Pas for any place else, they say. Like Thunder Bay, The Pas seems to have too many roads and shops for the population. There are a lot of travellers, though. My hotel has seventy rooms and it isn't short of customers. Why are all these people visiting this place? Or where are they driving to?

I am grounded until the starting problem is corrected. The plane lies at the dock, checked occasionally by curious muskrats. It was a fine dry day today, and I chafed at being on the ground. I had expected to be on the Coast by now.

Day Fifteen

July 10, 1990. Still grounded.

About half of the population here in The Pas is Indian. "All of them speak the Indian language," I was told. "Mostly Cree." Later, when I switched on the radio, I heard a Cree-language program. It sounded gutteral—like Chinese. (So, the Orient must be near, as all the early explorers had believed!)

Then I read, in a guide to The Pas, that this radio program had been started by Murray Mackenzie "of Scots-Métis and Cree Indian parents." (The Métis are of mixed blood, usually Scots-Indian or French-Indian.)

Mackenzie! I looked in the telephone book, but couldn't find Murray. I scanned the telephone book under "Native Organizations." They are an organized lot: Awasis Agency of No. Manitoba; Chemawawin First Nation; Flin Flon Indian Métis Friendship Association; Flin Flon Outreach; Grand Rapids Indian Band; Lyn Lake Friendship Centre; Manitoba Keewatinowi Okimakanak Inc.; Manitoba Métis Federation; Moose Lake Community Council; Moose Lake Indian Band; Swampy Cree Tribal Council; The Pas Friendship Centre; The Pas Indian Band. In my mind's eye, I saw the surrounding forests overrun by bands of Indians in business suits.

I decided to visit the Swampy Crees. The name had a gloomy, water-logged ring to it, and besides, it was the only name that was explicitly Cree, the same tribe as Murray Mackenzie. I went out onto the street, hailed a taxi, and gave the driver the address. "That's the shopping mall across the river you want," he said. The driver was an Indian (or a Métis? I couldn't tell). "Do you work for the circus?" he asked.

He had to be pulling my leg. Did I really look like I was recruiting for Buffalo Bill's Wild West Show? Well, it seemed that a travelling circus really had come to town and it was my Sears work shirt, the one that had gotten the evil eye in Quebec, that had identified me, a stranger, as a manual worker most likely connected to the circus.

We drove across the river and went into the shopping mall. There was no sign of the Swampy Cree Tribal Council. I stopped in a barber shop and asked the proprietor, who was a Métis, where the Swampy Cree were, and he said "We are all Indians. You are on the reservation. This mall is a reservation. All Indian-run."

The barber finished the haircut and the customer got up without paying. Hoping that haircuts were free, I sat down in the chair. While he cut my hair, the Métis—who was a very civil fellow—answered my questions about the Indians.

"The fur business has collapsed because of Greenpeace. They were even up here once," he said ruefully.

"What other problems do the Indians have?" I asked.

"The Treaty Indians just want their rights," he said, without elaboration.

He finished the haircut and charged me ten dollars. I had been "scalped" and didn't need a haircut for four months.

The customer who hadn't paid was still hanging around, listening to the conversation. He offered me a ride back over the river.

"What do you all do in The Pas?" I asked.

"Most people work at the mill. And we've got the biggest jail in the north. That's where I work."

"What do they get put away for?"

"Mostly alcohol-related crimes. And selling liquor on dry reserves."

Late this evening I telephoned Carolyn.

"Where were you when you called the other night?" she asked.

"Lake Winnipeg."

"Do you realize that you didn't make any sense? And that was my mother you talked to? I had already gone to bed. I thought you were flying across Canada, not boozing across. You ought to come home."

Any further prosecution of the voyage was now considered by them as altogether hopeless and impractical . . . I therefore employed those arguments which were best calculated to calm their immediate discontents, as well as to encourage their future hopes, though at the same time, I delivered my sentiments in such a manner as to convince them that I was determined to proceed. (Mackenzie, *Voyages*.)

Day Sixteen

July 11, 1990. As soon as Roy Boyes had fixed my airplane's generator (for that was the cause of the starting problem that had bedevilled me since Baltimore), I got ready to leave. About eleven o'clock I started my take-off run on the glassy water at the west end of Grace Lake and planed across the surface, then encountered some wind ripples which helped unstick the heavy little Cessna and transfer her weight, imperceptibly, from pontoons to wings.

Once off the water I climbed all the way up to eight hundred feet and followed the Saskatchewan River west as it meandered through the poorly drained green muskeg, dotted with algae-covered lakes and ponds.

... the Saskatchewine may be considered as navigable to near its source in the rocky mountains, for canoes, and without a carrying-place, making a great bend to Cumberland House.... (Mackenzie, *Voyages*.)

The route of Mackenzie and the voyageurs from The Pas to Churchill Lake was all upstream, by way of the Saskatchewan, Sturgeon-weir, and Churchill rivers. I planned to make this trip in two hops, stopping for fuel at Lac La Ronge, a place just off the canoe trunk line, but which is connected to the Churchill by its tributary, the Rapid River. Lac La Ronge, I read in Mackenzie, "has been an establishment for trade from the year 1782." That was the year Peter Pond wintered there, when he quarrelled with, and killed, another fur trader—an act that considerably affected Mackenzie's own career, for he was nominated to replace Pond.

Like most of the days I flew in Canada, the weather today was CAVU, or "ceiling and visibility unlimited." In Canada, the flying weather seems to be of two kinds: good or bad. There is much less of the in-between, hazy, thundery weather we have in Virginia, which gets its summer weather from the Gulf of Mexico.

Farther along the Saskatchewan, Cumberland House was visible from some distance away. It was Hudson's Bay's first inland post, and it had taken that slow-moving company a hundred years—until 1774—to move away from the Bay. Cumberland House also became an important provisioning place for Mackenzie's North West Company, a welcome resting place for the hard-paddling voyageurs.

Cumberland House appeared as a group of white buildings surrounded by green and yellow marsh. Flying nearer, I saw it to be a village-sized settlement of about one hundred houses set in a flat landscape. Once entirely dependent on water connections, the "miserable but strategic site" now has an air strip and a secondary road to Prince Albert. But no seaplane anchorage was shown on the chart, so I overflew the place. Its present function is to house Indians who formerly hunted in the bush but are now marooned on the edge of Cumberland Lake, which is silting up from the effects of the Squaw Rapids Dam.

I turned north to pick up the Sturgeon-weir River and saw on the horizon an unexpectedly huge chimney, belching smoke: the mill town of Flin Flon. It was at once characteristic of the frontier economy and incongruous to the landscape. More immediately, though, it was a useful landmark.

The Sturgeon-weir River—just a creek in some places—winds through tall conifer forests; it is known as a wonderful river to canoe down, and a tough river to go up. As I viewed the Sturgeon-weir, some parts of the river were calm enough for algae; other parts roiled in rapids. Seen from the air—and this is a misleading observation for canoeists—these rapids did not appear very remarkable. From the air, perspective is enlarged, but detail lost. I tried, by flying low, to get the advantages of both, but it didn't always work.

At Amisk Lake, I was over the Canadian Shield again, the land of clouds, trees, and water. The trail followed the Sturgeon-weir through the Shield to the Frog Portage. This portage was the voyageurs' connection with the Churchill River, which flows for one thousand miles, from Lac La Loche to Hudson Bay.

From studying the chart, I had foreseen a problem in following the Churchill, which is more a series of connected lakes than a river—and those amidst a great wilderness of other, uncounted lakes. In other words, I couldn't make head or tail of the chart.

Who ever heard of a major river whose course is often completely camouflaged by a hundred thousand lakes? I suspected that searching out Frog Portage was a good way to get

lost. "All the country," explains Mackenzie, "is interspersed by lakes, hills, and rivers. . . ."

I nosed over this country a bit, then thought better of it, and decided to follow a highway (Route 106) to the west, keeping just south of the Churchill River (wherever it was) and the broken country of the Canadian Shield. I was awed by the vastness and loneliness of the landscape and impressed by the precariousness of my journey. The only living, moving things I could see were the white pelicans flying just below me. I suppose they navigate as I do, by landmarks. In the absence of these, though, the birds' built-in instincts take over. Birds don't need any of the artificial navigational crutches we must have. In October 1850, one of the relief expeditions searching for Sir John Franklin encamped on an island off the north coast of Baffin Island and sent a carrier pigeon home to Ayr, in Scotland. It travelled the three thousand miles in 120 hours, arriving safely without LORAN.

Lac La Ronge. The town and seaplane base are at the west end of the large lake. I circled once and approached over the town into a southeast wind. There was an immediate answer to my radio call, and I was directed to the Air Sask ramp. From there, they sent me to a mooring. One of their pilots rode out on my right float and picked up the mooring line from the buoy, and we took a boat back to the dock.

What is it that attracts us to the water? Herman Melville says, in *Moby Dick,* that it is

> . . . that same image [that Narcissus saw] we ourselves see in all rivers and oceans. It is the image of the ungraspable phantom of life; and this is the key to it all.

It is quite deep enough an explanation for me.

Within a half-hour after arriving in the harbor, I was in the adjoining hotel, in a room with a balcony overlooking my seaplane and with a view of the other side of the lake, twenty miles away. The temperature was perfect, the day refreshing: a pure, sunlit day, with the pleasant sound of the waves lapping against the shore.

Later today, the wind picked up and continues to blow at midnight. A yellow, three-quarters moon illuminates the choppy black water.

Days 17-20

Day Seventeen

July 12, 1990. During the night, the plane jumped her buoy, which was now between the floats. Fortunately the wind had not been gusty enough to capsize the little seaplane.

I left Lac La Ronge and set out for Lake Athabasca, with a refuelling stop planned at Buffalo Narrows on Churchill Lake. I flew up to the Churchill River, about twenty-five miles north, but failed almost immediately to follow its zigzag progress through the lakes—the first lake I followed had no outlet.

I picked up my bearings at Pinehouse Lake. From fifteen miles away the tiny town on its shore stood out in the landscape: a nondescript little place sitting on a slight eminence, reflecting the sun from its asbestos roofs and gravel roads—a little shining Jerusalem, an image unlikely to be sustained on the ground. Once past it, and looking back into the sun, the town became invisible.

Mackenzie directed many letters to this place to his cousin, Roderic, who was stationed here in 1786 and 1787. "Try and get Rackets [snow shoes]," he wrote. "There is no stirring without them."

The space of intervening time between me and Mackenzie seemed to reinforce the spaciousness of the landscape. I felt as though I were a million miles from nowhere.

Soon I came to Lac Île-a-la-Crosse, which is part of the Churchill River system, and, according to Mackenzie, "re-

Fort McMurray ← Clearwater R. → Methye

Peter Po
this Ina
in

Lac La Loche

La Loche R.

Peter Pond Lake

white spruce

The bush is flat, featureless, 90% coniferous forest with open glades of light green muskeg & scattered lakes

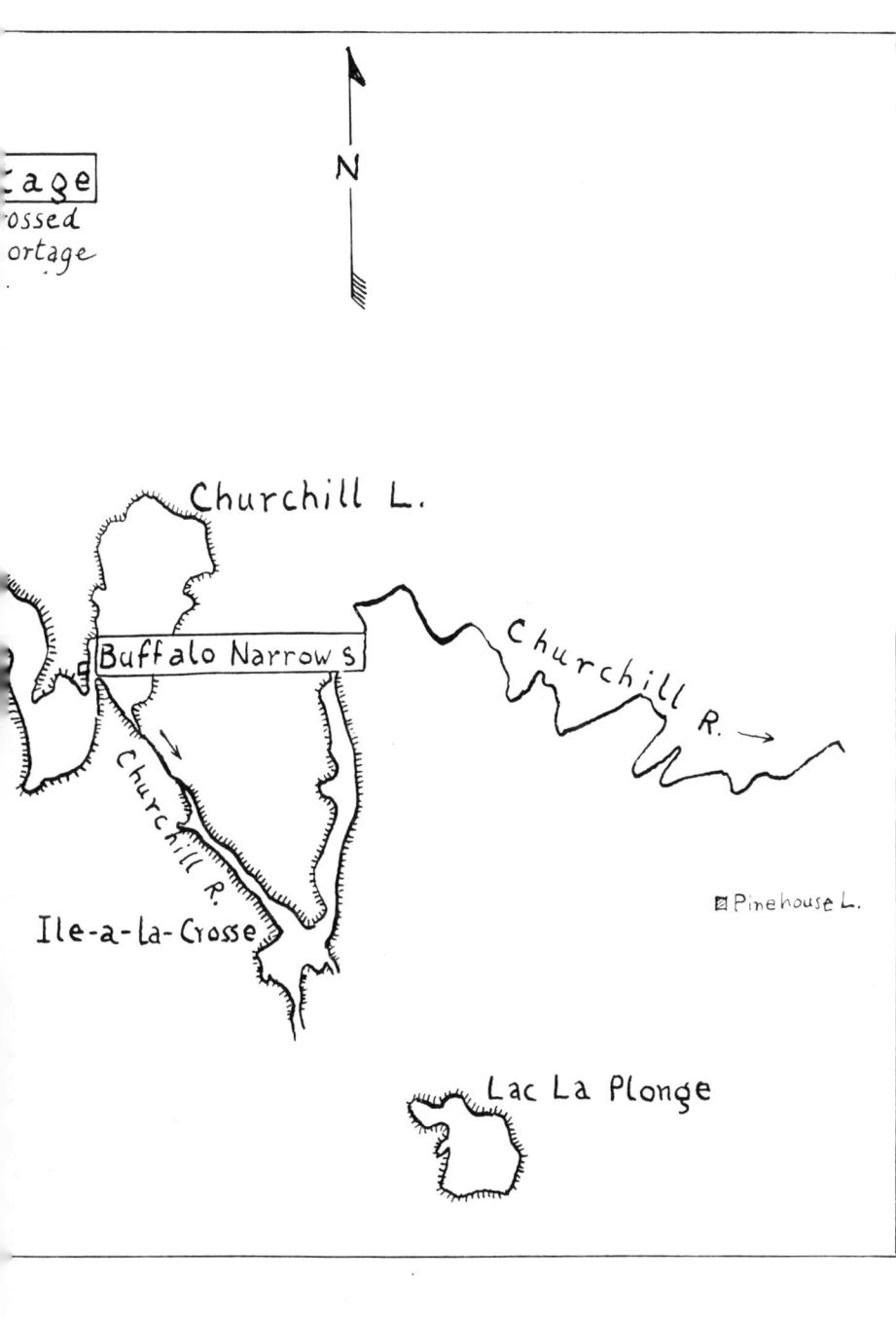

ceived its denomination from the game of the cross, which forms a principal amusement among the natives." When Mackenzie wrote that, he would have been well aware that, in 1763, the Indians captured Fort Mackinac by simulating a game of lacrosse outside its walls, and tricking the whites into opening a gate so that the ball could be retrieved, and the inhabitants massacred.

Lacrosse is a true North American invention, right up there with the airplane, the horse opera, ice hockey, Joseph Smith, drive-up divorce, affirmative action, "Hi!" and "O.K." Lacrosse is now mostly played by prep school teams. Too bad we cannot still see the game as it was once played, as George Catlin saw it and painted it—a wonderfully fluid picture of several hundred Choctaw Indians dressed in loin cloths and eagle-feather headdresses. (The sticks are similar to the ones used today.) Catlin's painting shows what looks more like a battle than a game, capturing the original vitality of a now-tired culture.

Forty miles up the Churchill, easily followed now for the river had left the Shield, I came to Buffalo Narrows. Its situation, next to "a narrow, crooked channel," Mackenzie describes as follows:

> ... [the river] opens to Lake Clear [Churchill Lake], which is very wide, and commands an open horizon, [then] by a narrow, crooked channel, turning to the South of West, the entry is made into Lake de Boeuf [Peter Pond Lake]... (Mackenzie, *Voyages*.)

Here I landed and tied up—with help—so that my tailplane projected safely beyond the rickety dock which was too high for it to clear. After I refuelled the plane, I telephoned Flight Service. They reported a line of thunderstorms near Fort McMurray. "It'll probably clear by four o'clock," they said.

"They're always forecasting thunderstorms that don't appear," grumbled the dispatcher.

While I was sitting on the dock, a passer-by stopped. "It's terrible what's happening at La Ronge," he said. "People are buying little blocks of property all around there. To me, it's just bush. You can't own it. People are losing their values. People call themselves Indians—the young ones—but they don't know how to live in the bush. What I want to do is to get some serious American hunters up here. Show 'em where the big bears are. It'll be nice. But it won't be cheap."

At 4:00 P.M. I called the weatherman again (he was two hundred miles away, in North Battleford); he thought it would be "O.K. to go." The sky was clear except for isolated, towering cumulus, he said. But I took another look at the lake and decided that the wind was now too strong here at Buffalo Narrows, where there were whitecaps in the harbor. I remembered Mike Forster saying, "If there are whitecaps on the water, there's too much wind to operate a small seaplane."

The dispatcher said, "You'll probably have to sell the plane here."

I am going "against the grain" of Canadian bush flying—going east-west instead of north-south. Bush flying is a north-south affair because its business is to service underdeveloped areas in the north from trade centers in the south. There is little call to fly east or west. Then, too, bush flying demands detailed knowledge of a specific area, so that pilots can fly in poor weather without radio aids. To the pros, I am following a seemingly haphazard westward path with which they never concern themselves, by a method strictly foreign to them, which is: I only fly when conditions are perfect, or nearly so.

The wind picked up force and my plane banged against the dock, for it was protected only by a couple of small flotation cushions I had brought along. I went down the road to a garage, cadged two bald tires, and hung them over the dock as bumpers, one at each end of the near float.

An osprey hovered overhead, hunting the lake.

After securing the airplane, I checked into the motel which is situated on a little isthmus between Peter Pond Lake and Churchill Lake. "This is Churchill Lake, then?" I asked the clerk.

"Don't know," he answered.

"How long have you been here?"

"Eleven years." He smiled complacently.

Day Eighteen

Buffalo Narrows. Friday, July 13, 1990. Grounded. A hot, windy day. Eighty-six degrees Fahrenheit. Whitecaps on the water. I walked up and down the town's few streets, and for want of anything else to do, ended up back at the café.

The Frenchman's Tale

"I married a Cree woman. She couldn't speak English at the time. French either. We had four children, two boys and two girls. She was just fine except when she drank. One night—it was forty-five below—she said, 'I think I'll go over to the bar for a drink. You stay home with the kids.' That was O.K. with me. Everyone needs an outing. Well, they must have got her worked up over there because, when they closed at 1:00 A.M., she came back to the house and announced her return by throwing a wash tub in through the front window.

"It isn't easy to get new windows at one o'clock in the morning. They don't think about that. I tried to put a blanket over the window to keep the cold out. The kids were crying. She wasn't helping any. In fact, she kept pulling the blanket down. I could have knocked her out, I suppose. But I don't hold with hitting a woman, so I called the RCMP. She kicked the windshield out of the van on the way to the lock-up.

"Alcohol? This is a town of thirteen hundred people that needs nine RCMP. What does that tell you? Ninety-five percent of the crime is alcohol-related. Half the treaty money and half the welfare is spent on booze. It isn't uncommon for the bar next door to take in ten thousand dollars in a single evening, when the checks come in. There's no bank in town, so why wouldn't they cash them here? [Note: the bar took in seven thousand dollars the following evening.] Then they bum cigarettes and try to charge everything 'til the next check comes. Well, there's nothing to do here. Half the town is unemployed year-round and ninety percent without jobs in the winter."

Day Nineteen

Buffalo Narrows. Saturday, July 14, 1990. The wind still blew today. Main Street was deserted except for a solitary raven hopping along the center of the road. The wind veered to the northwest and picked up strength, gusting to twenty-eight knots.

My plane was now tail-on to the wind. Wind gusts pushed down on the spring-loaded flaps from behind, causing them to bang up and down. The airplane jerked around on its lines, feeling the powerful need to weathercock into the wind. I was hesitant about turning the plane around in that wind, but one of the seaplaners said, "It's O.K. You can hold her on a line like a pet dog on a leash." We turned the plane into wind, and she lay calmly against the dock.

Showers and low clouds were expected all day. Nothing for it but to go back to the café.

A Trapper's Complaints

"Beavers? Reintroduced here in the 1940's. Brought in by seaplanes and released by letting them jump off the floats into the water. Now there are too many beavers. They've dammed ninety percent of the rivulets emptying into Lake Churchill. But they're not worth trapping anymore. Four years ago, I got sixty-eight dollars for a beaver pelt. Now it's down to ten dollars.

"Fish? The lakes were fished out for lack of any control. In the 1930's, Peter Pond Lake produced one million pounds of fish a year. Some of the Indians still fish. They put out their nets and make six hundred dollars in a day or two. Then they go and booze all the money away, and come back three days later and there's all those dead fish in the nets. They have to throw 'em away, eh!

"Pemmican? Never heard of it. Moose meat, you say? I shot a moose a few years back, and gave it to my wife to cut into strips and dry over a fire while I went fishing. Next thing I knew, she'd burned down the whole island!

"La Loche? Don't go there. They'll steal your plane and anything else you've got by the end of the day. It's that kind of town. Not like this place, Buffalo Narrows—you won't find a more respectable town in the North than this."

When the trapper had finished, the door to the café swung open, and in strode a constable of the RCMP, manly in bearing, smart in his pressed uniform and polished leather holster flap. Silence fell in the cafe. The Indians and the drunks and the rest of us stared at the constable like schoolboys staring at their headmaster.

The constable went up to the unshaven cook who, elbows on the counter, was dragging on a cigarette. "Come with me," said the constable in a low voice, jerking his head towards the door. They went out and, through the window, we could see them on the sidewalk. The constable was lecturing the cook, who returned, crestfallen.

"What did he want? You in trouble?" we asked.

"He said the egg-and-bacon sandwich he took out of here this morning crumbled all over the front of his uniform, and he had to go back to the barracks to change, and it better not happen again."

Day Twenty

Sunday, July 15, 1990. Another overcast morning, and the northwest wind did not diminish. I should be on my way back from the Pacific by now. I went to the bar and sat at a table. An Indian came and sat next to me, introducing himself as McDonald.

"I'm a Chip [Chipewyan]. I got two wives and nine children."

"Is it a secret?"

"No, they're all right here in town."

"They're not jealous of each other?"

"No. They both treat me very well. Hey, I'm supporting fifteen children and my first wife that left me six years ago. Here comes one of them now."

One of the wives approached McD, without apparent enthusiasm, and shook hands with him. She had a stocky build and wore a sweat shirt saying "Couch Potato."

> Plurality of wives is common [among the Chipewyan], and the ceremony of marriage is of a very simple nature. (Mackenzie, *Voyages*.)

"Isn't it expensive to heat three houses in the winter?" I asked McD.

"Don't cost me anything. The D.I.A. [Department of Indian Affairs] pays." He looked around the room. "Know why everyone around here likes me?"

"Why?"

"I pay all my bills at the end of the month. They love me at the grocery store."

McD drank his beer and walked away, leaving me to imagine how it once was.

"A hundred million years ago, a precautious North America stole away from Europe, drifted away to the west (she is still moving, scientists say, at the rate of 1/2 inch each year). After some eons more, she attained her full maturity: her extensive broad-leaved forests, her limitless prairies, her pure rivers, her countless fishes, her huge and varied flocks of birds and families of animals. In this state, North America thrived for millions of years, inhabited only by a few Stone-Age Indians, inconspicuous among her other fauna. It was God's Country."

Mckay, an old Indian befuddled with drink, came in and sat at the next table, next to a handsome white woman (correction: a Métis, who was identified as having an Irish grandfather). "Gi'me ten dollars," said the Indian, with an oath. "Wash your mouth out with soap," she said, but with no trace of anger. Then she said, to no one in particular, "This is God's country. Nobody else wants it."

Evening. An Otter airplane flew in and landed on the lake. I walked over to the dock, to watch the chief pilot bring her in. He cut the engine on the windward side of the jetty and drifted tail-first back towards it. He got out of the cockpit, walked unhurriedly back along the left float, stepped ashore before the plane touched, and swung the airplane alongside the dock. I dream of being that good.

Tomorrow I will follow Peter Pond's route to Athabasca. Pond was a fur trader, "an observing, enterprising, unprincipled Indian trader" according to John Bigsby, and a key figure in crossing the continent; a visionary frontiersman who found that the farther he travelled, the more he profited. Barely literate, yet an amateur mapmaker, his goal was to reach the Pacific, to profit from the sea otters reported by Captain Cook.

He was born in Milford, Connecticut, quite near to my stop on the Connecticut River, and served in the Army in the French and Indian Wars, before becoming a fur trader. He got as far west as Fort Chipewyan before he became *persona non grata* to his employer, the North West Company, for killing a rival fur trader there in 1788. He had already killed a trader at Lac La Ronge. He was replaced by the younger Mackenzie, who took up Pond's ambitions to explore the Northwest.

Days 21–23

🛩＊ Day Twenty-One

*J*uly 16, 1990. Slam. Bam. The little airplane recoiled from the bruising waves of Lake Churchill and fled north to Peter Pond Lake. Sped off to Mackenzie's Northwest headquarters.

🛶 It was named Fort Chepewyan, and is in latitude 58.38 North, longitude 110.26 West. (Mackenzie, *Voyages*.)

Mackenzie went north from Buffalo Narrows alongside the pebble beach of Peter Pond Lake, and up the La Loche River. Then, across Lac La Loche and over the long Methye Portage; then down the Clearwater and the Athabasca rivers to Fort Chipewyan on Lake Athabasca. This is the route he took, and I set out to follow him.

At least as big and as blue as Lake Geneva, Peter Pond Lake is connected to Lac La Loche (Methye Lake) by the La Loche River, which is barely a creek along some parts of its course.

🛶 At the North-West end [Peter Pond Lake] receives the waters of the river La Loche, which, in the fall of the year, is very shallow, and navigated with difficulty even by half-laden canoes. Its water is not sufficient to form strong rapids, though from its rocky bottom the canoes are frequently in considerable danger. (Mackenzie, *Voyages*)

At the north end of Peter Pond Lake, I saw a stone cairn which I supposed to mark the beginning of this longest portage of the entire canoe route from Montreal to Fort Chipewyan. The Methye Portage extended thirteen miles, mostly through scrub pine, and formed the fur traders' link with the Clearwater River, a tributary of the Athabasca.

> This portage is the ridge that divides the waters which discharge themselves into Hudson's Bay, from those that flow into the Northern Ocean. . . . The Portage La Loche is of a level surface, in some parts abounding with stones, but in general it is an entire sand, and covered with the cypress, the pine, the spruce fir, and other trees natural to its soil. (Mackenzie, *Voyages*.)

Two-thirds of the way across the portage, I came to Rendezvous Lake, where I could see the trail running down to a sandy beach.

This spot was a transhipment point for the Hudson's Bay Company. Unlike the North West Company, HBC did not carry its boats across this portage, but used two sets of boats, one set at each end. Only the cargoes (furs from the north, trade goods from the east) were carried across the portage and exchanged at the rendezvous; the voyageurs were spared the labor of carrying the boats.

This portage was in use for about one hundred years; until 1885 and completion of the Canadian Pacific Railway five hundred miles south, the Methye Portage was still the fastest way to cross Canada.

Now, as I flew overhead, all was still. I sensed a brooding silence even over the noise of my engine.

The portage trail, now hidden to me under the trees, led down a steep escarpment into the valley of the Clearwater. This, I thought, was a very attractive river, particularly so on a sunny day like this, with the earth dappled in cloud shadows. The river wasn't very wide and not at all clear, having brownish waters, but it flowed through a valley of picturesque wooded slopes; and the river itself alternately cascaded down rocky gorges in rapids and waterfalls or meandered between shining sand bars.

Describing the scene, Mackenzie went one better.

This precipice . . . commands a most extensive, romantic, and ravishing prospect. From thence the eye looks down on the course of the little river, by some called the Swan river, and by others, the Clear-Water and Pelican river, beautifully meandering for upwards of thirty miles. The valley, which is at once refreshed and adorned by it, is about three miles in breadth and is confined by two lofty ridges of equal height, displaying a most beautiful intermixture of wood and lawn, and stretching on till the blue mist obscures the prospect. (Mackenzie, *Voyages*.)

It is a passage, most likely embellished by his editor, that reflects the late-eighteenth century enthusiasm for nature popularized by the poet Wordsworth.

I followed the Clearwater to the point where it flows into the Athabasca. There was Fort McMurray below me, a large town for the North, with a landing area on the river that I had been warned to avoid. From there, I flew north down the Athabasca River, past the tar sands mentioned by Mackenzie. This deposit is supposed to have reserves of three hundred billion barrels of oil in the saturated sands.

Beneath me was the Athabasca, a wide, muddy river, flowing through a hundred thousand square miles of wilderness. Lowering clouds now covered all the sky, and it was comforting to fly along the big river, knowing that I could not get lost following it. Still, I opened the throttle to get to Fort Chipewyan as soon as I could. There was little traffic on the river—a barge, the odd seaplane—and only the occasional tiny settlement on its banks. Rain showers blotted out the western end of Lake Athabasca from view, so instead of flying there direct, I approached Fort Chipewyan from the east.

As I got closer I saw the town, tucked into the western end of this huge lake and sheltered somewhat by a fringe of rocky, tree-covered islands. The chart marked a seaplane landing area on Lake Athabasca in front of the town (though I saw no planes there), but I had already determined to go to the more sheltered alighting area on Small Lake just northeast of town. There I set my plane down. There was one seaplane at the dock. I taxied towards it and was happy to see a man come out to meet me. "Are you Mark?"

"Yes."

"I talked to you on the phone," I said.

"Yes. We've had lousy weather for the last two days. Rain, and thirty knot winds."

Mark drove me over to The Lodge, a hotel almost empty of guests, on a granite outcrop overlooking Lake Athabasca, a yellow sea under a dismal sky. Next to the Lodge, on another rocky outcrop, there was a cairn memorializing the site of the Hudson's Bay Company's fur-trading post, and below it, a reconstruction of a wooden warehouse which serves as a museum. (Mackenzie's post was across the water, on the south side of the lake, where it was occupied until 1798.)

"About the only thing worth seeing in Fort Chip is the Chinese waitress at the Athabasca Café," said Mark.

(Always, this fixation with the Orient. But the Orient wasn't to be found by a Northwest Passage, although Franklin himself passed this way in 1820, in search of it. The Chinese waitress: is she a compensating image for the vanished dream of reaching the Orient? I will soon find out.)

Day Twenty-Two

Fort Chipewyan. July 17, 1990. A dismal day, rainy and cold.

"Fort Chip," as it is called by the locals, is a small, raw town set in a bleak Scottish-type landscape.

Fort Chip is not connected overland to anywhere by road, except by snow road in winter; instead, access is by air or water. Despite the superabundance of fresh water, there is none available to drink today, and the restaurants, two or three in number, are closed because the town water supply has become polluted. The reasons were not made clear to me, but it seems that high water levels on the Athabasca River have something to do with it, bringing industrial pollutants downstream from Fort MacMurray. Anyway, the restaurants are closed, and the glory of the town, the Chinese waitress, must remain a traveller's tale.

Fort Chip, isolated though it is, is a completely urban environment with autos, telephones, videos, a laundromat. And—this is the thing that would really surprise Alexander Mackenzie—everyone lives in town. In Mackenzie's time, and up to less than fifty years ago, the Indians lived in the bush and came to town only occasionally.

The population of this place is about fifteen hundred persons. The latest figures I could find were for 1982. Then, it was ninety-two percent Indian ("42% Cree, 34% Metis, 16% Chipewyan"). A 1959 visitor reported, "The population is about five hundred Indians—Crees and Chipewyans—and twenty whites, but the Indian population is very mobile, many of them spending part of the year in the bush and part living in tents in town." I saw no tents here today.

Almost no one works regularly in Fort Chip, except for a few government employees. The fur trade is all but dead, hurt by the slump in demand; hurt, too, by the hydro-electric dam, nine hundred miles up the Peace River, which eliminated the spring flooding on the delta at Fort Chip and damaged the habitat of muskrat and beaver.

What of the fishing industry?

🛶 The fishery requires the most unremitting attention, as the voyaging Canadians are equally indolent, extravagant, and improvident, when left to themselves, and rival the savages in a neglect of the morrow. The nets are visited every day, and taken out every other day to be cleaned and dried. This is a very ready operation when the waters are not frozen, but when . . . the ice has acquired its greatest thickness, which is sometimes as much as five feet, holes [must be] cut in it. . . Thus do these voyagers live, year after year, entirely upon fish. . . . (Mackenzie, *Voyages*.)

The fishing industry spoken of by Mackenzie is moribund. In the summer of 1990, there were only five fishermen operating from Fort Chip. I was told, "The rest got discouraged by low prices and storm damage to the nets. But if you can get any sort of seasonal employment for twenty weeks—fire fighting or construction—you qualify for unemployment checks for the rest of the year. The Treaty Indians get their entitlements anyway."

It is generally said here that the problem with the Canadian inland fishing industry is over-fishing. The provincial governments overdid it with their policies of encouraging seine-netting and putting up freezer plants. So what happened to all the slow-growing northern fish? Fished out.

A gloomy day, yet summer. How could Mackenzie have put up with this place for eight years? (For one thing, he had two thousand books at the post. For another, he was travelling on the fur business much of the time.)

Fort Chip, at latitude 58.43 N, is one of a handful of Canadian towns situated above latitude fifty-five north. Considerably less than one percent of Canada's population lives in the seventy-five percent of her territory that is located north of that line. It's too cold up here. For six months of the year, there are more Canadians in Florida and the West Indies than in the Canadian North.

Latitude fifty-five north is near to the southern boundary of the permafrost line, a discontinuous, patchy line which includes the greater part of Canada's land surface, from sixty north in the far West to fifty-one north in Labrador.

The frozen subsoil of the permafrost region may be forested or carpeted with mosses, lichens, grasses, and dwarf shrubs. But the land is useless for farming and costly to build on. For much of the year the weather is very cold. At Fort Chip, I am told, the lake is frozen to a depth of five feet in winter.

Only the Indians could feel at home in this place. The white man is ill-adapted to it. It's different with birds and mammals. A glance at the range maps in the *Peterson Field Guide to Birds* shows that an enormous number of bird species live and breed even in the farthest parts of the North, as far as the huge, remote Arctic islands of Baffin, Victoria, and Elizabeth. Year-round residents there include the raven, grouse, ptarmigan, and snowy owl; summer breeders include a host of geese, ducks, warblers and other birds. The area around Fort Chip is home, for at least part of the year, to 226 species of birds, 45 different mammals, and 20 species of fish.

Day Twenty-Three

Fort Chipewyan, July 18, 1990. Still grounded.

Of the Chipewyan, Mackenzie writes: "peaceable, sober,

timorous, and vagrant. Complexion is swarthy; their features coarse, nor have they the piercing eye. . . . Not addicted to spirituous liquors."

Of the Cree (Mackenzie calls them by their French name, the Knisteneaux): "warlike; colder, more reserved than the Chipewyan. Well proportioned. Their eyes are keen and penetrating."

I decided to conduct my own survey of these matters. Of the first convenient Indian, I asked, "What is the difference between a Chip and a Cree?"

"I'm a Cree. I'm married to a Chip. There's no difference. We're one family."

"Is the language different?"

"Yes."

"Can you speak Chip?"

"Yes."

"Are there any recognizable differences between the two peoples?"

(Puzzled) "No."

Separately, I took this up with a white resident. "There is a difference between Chip and Cree," he said. "Not in looks. The Chip is a little more open to communication than the Cree, who is difficult to get across to."

"Try stubborn," said a second white.

Of all the Indian nations, the Cree women are the most comely. (Mackenzie, *Voyages*)

"Oh, Yes!" said a pilot. "Some of the Cree girls are good looking. I'm working on one right now. It's slow. I'm taking her up this afternoon for a flying lesson."

Elsewhere in town, I was told:

"Fort Chip doesn't have a liquor store but there are nineteen bootleggers. A native can drink five or six 26-ounce bottles of whisky in a night. I've seen a man drunk for ten days at a stretch. That doesn't include the hangover period."

After the first European contact with North America, it was fashionable to depict the Indian as a noble savage. Man in a state of nature was supposed to have been free, healthy, honest and happy, but man in society had been corrupted and enslaved. Mackenzie, who followed trade practice and supplied the Indians with rum, subscribed in part to this belief:

> It will appear from the fatal consequences I have repeatedly imputed to the use of spirituous liquors that I more particularly consider these people [the Cree] as having been, morally speaking, great sufferers from their communication with the subjects of civilised nations. (Mackenzie, *Voyages.*)

The stranger, the traveller, is confronted with two myths—or, rather, extreme views—of the Red Indian: the old romantic myth, based on the tales of James Fenimore Cooper, and the other view of the Indian as eternally drunk and existing on perpetual welfare.

"The Government will buy them a new house every five years. Why? Because the natives are very destructive. If they need wood for the fire, they'll take a chain saw to the house."

I was eager to see and report on such an innovation. (If it is O.K. to chain-saw a tree, why not a house?). But my investigations resulted only in a conversation about rhubarb, with an Indian whom I came upon while he was hoeing his garden. There was something familiar about all this, and I searched Mackenzie's book.

⚓ In the fall of the year 1787, when I first arrived at Athabasca, Mr. Pond was settled on the banks of the river, where he remained for three years, and had formed as fine a kitchen garden as I ever saw in Canada. (Mackenzie, *Voyages*.)

Earlier in the day, I went to check on my seaplane and found that I had left the master switch on, and run down the battery. I asked around town about a battery recharger. An Indian offered to hook up my battery on his front porch. This evening I went and collected the recharged battery.

"I'd like to have seen the traditional dress at the pow wow," I said.

"Traditional dress?" said the Indian. "There's none around here. Must have come with the band we hired."

11:00 P.M. A light grey sky over the metallic lake.

Days 24–26

![icon] *Day Twenty-Four*

*J*uly 19, 1990. What a letdown! I awoke to find the sky still gray, and low clouds scudding overhead. I wasn't going anywhere until the weather was good and ready. I foresaw an inconsequential day ahead, a walk to the laundromat and back in the rain. By 9:00 A.M., though, the forecast made good and the sky started to clear from the west. I hurriedly packed my things to leave.

![icon] October 10, 1792. Having made every necessary preparation, I left Fort Chepewyan, to proceed up the Peace River. I had resolved to go as far as our most distant settlement, which would occupy the remaining part of the season, it being the route by which I proposed to attempt my next discovery, across the mountains from the source of that river. (Mackenzie, *Voyages*.)

I went down to my toy airplane on its little lake. I was playing a bit part in a John Ford movie, in which the characters and action are dwarfed by the immensity of the landscape. Small Lake, a pond really, when compared to anything much, and especially Lake Athabasca, was said to be 4,700 feet in length, but it didn't look that long. The lake is peanut-shaped and, from the dock, I couldn't see around the bend, so it looked even smaller. When I taxied away from the corner where the dock is, though, I could see down the full length of the little lake to the unobstructed far end, which leads into the delta of the Peace.

The air was calm, so I would get no help from the wind, but no hindrance from a cross wind or tail wind. My plane was still overloaded, though I'd sent home twenty pounds of books and charts by parcel post—but what were twenty pounds of books compared to the 180 pounds of reserve fuel that I was carrying? I always carry a full load of fuel, regardless of the length of the flight—it gives me extra time to find the way.

I taxied to the corner of the lake, faced the far end, and opened the throttle. I put the plane on the step, simultaneously trimming her nose down so that she planed over the water surface, building up speed. After she settled into this mode, I trimmed back to lighten the load on the yoke, and rocked her sideways—not fore and aft, as has been my practice—and she flew smoothly off the end of the lake, heading west. I was again on Mackenzie's trail to the sea, with full tanks, charts for the route, emergency gear, and grab lines streaming from the struts.

Fort Chip was the jumping-off point for Mackenzie's expedition to the Pacific. Tracking him from Fort Chipewyan would take me up the Peace River to the Rocky Mountains and over the divide to the River of the West.

I followed the Peace River, a grand, muddy river, upstream to the west. On either side was the bush, a poorly-drained, haphazard arrangement of conifers, aspens, dwarf pines, and hundred-acre velvet glades. Here the Peace meandered through flat country, with a steep bank on the outside of the river bend and a sandy beach on the inside.

Below me was Wood Buffalo National Park, a 17,500 square-mile tract, home to about five thousand bison; the last honest-to-goodness home to the remnants of herds that once numbered sixty million. I kept a lookout but didn't spot even one of them.

By a combination of luck and good judgement, the Canadians managed to preserve a small number of wood and plains buffalo that have increased to their present numbers. Is this a happy ending? Or should we focus on the sixty million that were killed in North America, and the fate of any other thing marginally useful to man? It is a preoccupation of our time that Mackenzie didn't have—and I don't want. I would rather not know all this; I would rather enjoy flying over North America, free as a bird, secure in the belief that Canada, at least, is too big to be entirely trashed.

I flew along a broad avenue in the sky, between banks of clouds on north and south horizons, towards a perfectly clear western horizon. There was little sign of life, just a few logged tracts and the occasional settlement. Of some settlements marked on the chart, I saw no sign. Place names on Canadian maps tend to be optimistic; the only remaining evidence of one town that is still named on the map is said to be an old bath tub. But there is a lot of empty space to fill on the map of Canada and it is not unexpected, perhaps, that a twelve-inch globe, which omits Chattanooga, Tennessee and Nottingham, England, should show Fort Vermilion, Alberta, a tiny town that just happens to be in a big open space.

Now, Mackenzie's trail was easy to follow. After an hour's flying, I came to Vermilion Chutes, a hamlet of five cabins. I passed low over the falls he reported, white water sliding over a wide limestone ledge that the aeronautical chart identified as: Vermilion Falls 25′.

> October 17, 1792. At three in the afternoon . . . we arrived at the falls. The river at this place is about four hundred yards broad, and the fall about twenty feet high. . . On the morning of the 18th, as soon as we got out of the draught of the fall, the wind being at North-East, and strong in our favour, we hoisted sail, which carried us on at a considerable rate against the current. . . (Mackenzie, *Voyages*.)

The character of the Peace River is both aloof and unambiguous. Aloof, because its banks are largely uninhabited and its waters scarcely travelled; unambiguous because, after the sometimes convoluted routes of Canadian waterways, the Peace flows directly across northern Canada, passing boldly through the silent country.

Two hours out from Fort Chip, approaching Fort Vermilion in rain showers, I crossed some fields of bright yellow rape, then fields of mown hay. My original plan had included refuelling at Fort Vermilion, an old settlement located on the Peace River, at the point just before the Peace makes a ninety degree turn to the south. But I had found, through a succession of telephone calls made yesterday, that fuel was available only at a place called Footner Lake. Located near the town of High Level, this lake is about thirty-five miles from the place on the Peace River bend where Mackenzie spent three nights in October 1792.

At six o'clock in the morning of the 20th, we landed before the house amidst the rejoicing and firing of the people, who were animated with the prospect of again indulging themselves in the luxury of rum. . . . (Mackenzie, *Voyages*.)

I might have gone on today, farther along the Peace to Fort St. John, but the forecast was for cumulus build-up for the rest of the day, then drier air the next day, Friday. So I'm staying here tonight, in the town of High Level.

This evening, wanting to confirm the weather outlook, I switched on the television and was confronted by a seer from Edmonton. Making invocations to a synoptic chart, he uttered a Delphic outlook: ". . . a stationary mother low on the Pacific coast is spawning little lows that will move east over northern Alberta." But what about the weather?

Day Twenty-Five

July 20, 1990. A fine day. I left Footner Lake and headed south. Beyond Fort Vermilion, the Peace River takes a pretty decisive heading south, flowing in a valley about five miles wide. Flying south up the Peace, I saw that the river flows between increasingly steeper banks. There are sporadic cultivations along the west bank, but the country to the east is a wilderness.

Eventually, the Peace bends west, and is joined by the Smoky River, at a place of sandy bars and islands. It was near here that Mackenzie made his winter camp, 1792/3.

It was also near here, in 1920, that "Wop" May set up a base camp to prospect for oil—by air—along the Great Slave Lake and the Mackenzie River. He was flying for an oil company that sent two Junkers airplanes from New York to Peace River for this purpose.

"Wop" May was a colorful character whose wartime career included—on his first time out—an air fight with Manfred von Richthofen. The Red Baron couldn't let this one go. It would be too easy—his eighty-first victim. He got greedy. Ignoring his own rules, he followed May's Sopwith Camel low over the allied lines. Then another Canadian, Captain Roy Brown, got on the German's tail and killed him.

It was in the twenties, too, that aerial prospector Jack Caldwell came this way searching for a lost gold strike in the Barrens. An old prospector had showed up in Calgary with a jar full of high-grade gold quartz, and got the backing of a syndicate to work the lode. He wouldn't tell them the location, but offered to take a party to the place, which was marked by rocks shaped in the form of a giant cross. But the prospector used his advance money to go on a drinking spree in Calgary and was hit over the head with a bottle during a brawl. The blow affected his memory and he could not recall the exact spot of his find. By now the syndicate had purchased a Vickers Viking amphibian, and they decided to go ahead and have Caldwell search for the gold. The plane was shipped by rail to Lac La Biche, and from there Caldwell took it north for two months, but with no success.

By the end of the 1920's, the use of airplanes, especially seaplanes, was widespread throughout Canada. It was a time of "Flying a six-day canoe trip in half an hour," and "Lakes more than a hundred miles long seen from the air which are not yet shown on the map."

This far down the Peace, Mackenzie was in undiscovered territory, and from now on he would rely on the planet Jupiter, low on the southern night horizon, not as a lodestar to direct his course, but rather to record it. It was by Jupiter, and observation of its satellites, that he would determine his longitude and validate his explorations. In those days, the only sure ways of fixing longitude were by observing Jupiter or by the method of lunar distances—both of them extremely cumbersome methods by the standards of today.

Mackenzie, on his trip overland to the Pacific, though he took a chronometer (an instrument demonstrated with great success by Captain Cook), depended on the then still-used method developed by Galileo to determine longitude. Galileo, who discovered the four largest satellites of the planet Jupiter in 1610, worked out a table of the times of their rotation and devised a method of determining longitude from those observations. In the account of his voyage to the Pacific, Mackenzie continually refers to establishing his longitude by observing the eclipses of the planet Jupiter's satellites. It is a pleasing thought that these satellites, whose discovery revolutionized our idea of space—everything did not revolve around earth—should also have served in the exploration of North America.

Mackenzie resumed his journey along the Peace River the following spring.

🛶 May 9, 1793. . . . the canoe was put into the water . . . [with] an equipage of ten people. . . With these persons I embarked at seven in the evening. We began our voyage with a course South by West against a strong current one mile and three quarters, South-West by South one mile, and landed before eight on an island for the night.

Except for the woods along the river's escarpments, the country beyond the junction of the Peace and the Smoky rivers is mostly or entirely cultivated prairie. It seemed to me a very benign place, with the sun shining on the green and yellow fields.

🛶 May 10, 1793. From the place we quitted this morning, the West side of the river displayed a succession of the most beautiful scenery I had ever beheld. The ground rises at intervals to a considerable height . . . at every interval or pause in the rise, there is a very gently ascending space or lawn. . . . This magnificent theatre of nature has all the decorations which the trees and animals of the country can afford it: groves of poplars in every shape vary the scene; and their intervals are enlivened with vast herds of elks and buffaloes. (Mackenzie, *Voyages*.)

Going west, half way to Fort St. John, I followed the Peace into higher country, to a point where the river is held tightly in its gorge. Hereabouts, Mackenzie's party first saw the Rocky Mountains.

🛶 May 17, 1793. At two in the afternoon, the rocky mountains appeared in sight, with their summits covered in snow, bearing South-West by South: they formed a very agreeable object to every person in the canoe, as we attained the view of them much sooner than we expected. (Mackenzie, *Voyages*.)

Three days later, at Peace River Canyon, Mackenzie came to the most extensive rapids on the Peace River: "the river above us, as far as we could see, was one white sheet of foaming water." It took him five days to portage around these rapids.

On May 31, 1793, three weeks after Mackenzie's party left their camp at the Smoky River, they reached the forks of the Peace, deep in the mountains. Mackenzie was hopeful that they had found a way through the Rocky Mountains, but:

> The view convinced us that our late hopes were without foundation, as there appeared a ridge or chain of mountains, running South and North as far as the eye could see.
> On advancing two or three miles, we arrived at the fork [of the Peace], one branch running about West-North-West, and the other South-South-East. If I had been governed by my own judgement, I should have taken the former, as it appeared to me to be the most likely to bring us nearest to the part where I wished to fall on the Pacific Ocean. . . (Mackenzie, *Voyages*.)

On the advice of an old Indian, Mackenzie followed the south fork (now known as the Parsnip), having been told that by doing so he would "arrive at the carrying place to another large river." That river Mackenzie supposed would lead to the Ocean.

I followed the Peace to Fort St. John, an old Hudson's Bay post, now a big town on the Alaska Highway, some 120 miles below the forks of the Peace. Near Fort St. John, I landed for fuel at Charlie Lake. The place was unattended except for a pilot who happened to be on the little dock; he helped me tie up and refuel the seaplane, then drove me to a telephone to file my flight plan to Tabor Lake, near the city of Prince George, the erstwhile fur-trading post of Fort George.

At 1:00 P.M. I took off from Charlie Lake. At this altitude (2,266 feet above sea level) and time of day, the engine did not pull quite so well in the thin air, and the plane was reluctant to get "on the step." Once in the air, I climbed over the Peace River gorge and headed west towards the mountains dead ahead. Flying a small plane really is like riding a magic carpet, and the wonder of sailing high over rivers, forests and mountains insufficiently explained by Bernoulli's Theorem of lifting surfaces.

At the gateway to the Rockies, I came upon the Bennett Dam. Its appearance jolted my illusion of having travelled up a free, remote river. The completion of the Bennett Dam on the Peace River created (at the forks of which Mackenzie writes) a huge "Y"-shaped lake, Williston Lake, whose arms are named Peace, Parsnip and Finlay reaches. The elevation of Lake Williston is 2,205 feet.

Here I entered the Rocky Mountains, in close pursuit of Mackenzie, who arrived at the Pacific this same day, July 20. I wasn't that far behind him.

The steep, snow-capped mountains towered to six or seven thousand feet on the sides of the blue lake, towered above my tiny seaplane as I flew towards the gorge at the west end. Zephyrs on the lake beyond funneled into a brisk breeze that rippled the waters in the gorge and rocked the little Cessna's wings.

The shores of the lake were littered with the debris of logging. I saw only two tiny boats on Peace Reach, but on Parsnip Reach there were numerous tugs towing logs to the mill at the town of Mackenzie. I saw no hawks or ducks or any bird over these waters.

I was now in British Columbia, a place well over twice the

size of California and with scenery and resources to scale. It is a place I knew only from photographs, "courtesy British Columbia Government Tourist Bureau": a Paul Bunyan land, the place of a single, grinning logger in a landscape of tree stumps, a proud midget, "felling a Douglas fir born with Magna Carta."

From the south end of Parsnip Reach I followed the Parsnip River upstream. To my eye, the Parsnip appeared green in color.

Mackenzie was at this same place, June 1, 1793. Later, on June 5, Mackenzie passed the tiny Pack River turnoff and continued up the Parsnip.

June 6, 1793. [Six days after passing the forks.] . . . we proceeded by hauling the canoe from branch to branch. The current was so strong, that it was impossible to stem it with the paddles; the depth was too great to receive any assistance from the poles, and the bank of the river was so closely lined with willows and other trees, that it was impossible to employ the line. (Mackenzie, *Voyages*.)

The country of the Parsnip is a rolling plateau, and from a high-flying airplane it should be possible to see where the Parsnip peters out at its source and where the Fraser River comes from the east and bends south towards the city of Prince George. I did not gain all this advantage from my low-flying seaplane, but did have a better idea of the country than did Mackenzie, who had no such view. Nor did he have the luxury, as I did, of landing here at Tabor Lake, just outside Prince George, where I secured my plane to the grassy bank, ordered a steak in an adjacent restaurant, and discovered, from looking closely at my chart, that I had lost Mackenzie's trail. Well, short-cut it.

I had unwittingly followed the more inviting valley of the

Pack and Crooked rivers, where it diverged from the valley of the Parsnip. I had flown straight south along the Crooked River to its source in Summit Lake, within sight of the Fraser. I had not been nearer than forty miles to the source of the Parsnip. This route, which I took by mistake, would have been a better way for Mackenzie to go.

There is no obvious route from the fork of the Peace River in the Rocky Mountains to the Pacific Ocean. It was difficult to follow the small reproduction of Mackenzie's map in the edition of his *Voyages* that I carried with me. Mackenzie's account was difficult to follow on this leg, too, because the rivers and lakes he described (such as the McGregor and the Fraser rivers; Arctic and Pacific lakes) were not named until later. And I did not have that information at hand at the time, only Mackenzie's own account. But with more careful preparation, I could have followed Mackenzie more closely.

Meanwhile, Mackenzie's party followed their tormented path along the wild rivers. They reached the source of the Parsnip at Arctic Lake on June 12, 1793, and then crossed the continental divide at nearby Pacific Lake. (This was the part I missed.) In starting down the Pacific slope of the Rockies, on Bad River, they had their worst accident.

> ... the violence of the current was so great as to drive her sideways down the river, and break her by the first bar, when I instantly jumped into the water, and the men followed my example; but before we could set her straight, we came to deeper water, so that we were obliged to reembark ... [and] we drove against a rock which shattered the stern of the canoe [so] that it held only by the gunwhales and the steersman could no longer keep his place. The violence of this stroke drove us to the opposite side of the river, which is but narrow, when the bow met with the same

fate as the stern . . . the steersman, who had not recovered from his fright, called out to his companions to save themselves. My peremptory commands superseded the effects of his fear, and they all held fast to the wreck . . . as we should otherwise have been dashed against the rocks by the force of the water, or driven over the cascades. (Mackenzie, *Voyages.*)

Mackenzie and his men repaired their canoe, made their way (via the McGregor) to the Fraser on the 17th of June, and tried that river long enough to realize that the going was impossible. The local Indians confirmed that the Fraser was impassible.

June 22, 1793. I now proceeded to request the native, whom I had particularly selected, to commence his information, by drawing a sketch of the country upon a large piece of bark, and he immediately entered on the work, frequently appealing to, and sometimes asking the advice of, those around him. He described the river as running to the East of South, receiving many rivers, and every six or eight leagues encumbered with falls and rapids, some of which were very dangerous, and six of them impracticable. (Mackenzie, *Voyages.*)

It was "still a long way to the sea" down this river (the Fraser), yet there was another way, "very short to the Western Ocean." Mackenzie reluctantly decided to go back up the Fraser and look for the alternative route described by the Indians. Going farther down the Fraser, he realized, even if it could be done, would mean running out of time.

I reflected on the tardy progress of my return up it . . . [and, if I went farther down the Fraser] I must give up every expectation of returning this season to Athabasca. (Mackenzie, *Voyages.*)

Now that Mackenzie had decided to abandon the plan of going south on the Fraser, he questioned the natives on the details of the alternative route they had spoken of.

> At the commencement of this conversation, I was very much surprised by the following question from one of the Indians: "What," demanded he, "can be the reason that you are so particular and anxious in your inquiries of us respecting a knowledge of this country: do not you white men know every thing in the world?" This interrogatory was so very unexpected, that it occasioned some hesitation before I could answer it. At length, however, I replied, that we certainly were acquainted with the principal circumstances of every part of the world; that I knew where the sea is, and where I myself then was, but that I did not exactly understand what obstacles might interrupt me in getting to it; with which, he and his relations must be well acquainted, as they had so frequently surmounted them. Thus I fortunately preserved the impression in their minds, of the superiority of white people over themselves. (Mackenzie, *Voyages.*)

When I called Carolyn this evening, she said, "I don't know how you think you're going to make it to Manhattan by the end of the month."

"Oh, we'll figure something out."

"What's this 'we,' white man?"

Day Twenty-Six

July 21, 1990. Tabor Lake. A clear night with bright stars slowly gave way to the dawn. A coyote howled on the opposite hill. The morning came clear and very still.

The surface of the lake was like glass, and I thought I

should wait for some wind. When it didn't come, I untied the mooring lines and silently paddled the always-overloaded seaplane away from the shore.

I started the engine, though reluctant to demolish the silence of the morning. The far shore of the lake looked quite near in the clear air, so I taxied to the near shore, in amongst the water lilies, opened the engine full, and forced the plane over onto the step. She skimmed across the smooth water and lifted herself into the air. Airborne, I turned back over the lake and looked down to see the waves from my wake on the water, where the seaplane had plowed along nose high at the beginning of its take-off run.

From Lake Tabor, I flew about fifty miles down the fast-flowing Fraser until I came to the West Road River.

> July 3, 1793. . . . at ten we came to a small river, which answered to the description of that whose course the natives said, they follow in their journies to the sea coast. . . . (Mackenzie, *Voyages*)

After turning back up the Fraser, Mackenzie and his men built a new canoe, and arrived, on July 3, at the junction of the Fraser River—it had not then received its name—with a lesser river Mackenzie named the "West-road River." Following this river, he had learned from the Indians, would take them to "the lake of nauseous water"—the ocean.

My aeronautical chart showed Mackenzie's West Road River, and it showed his "Stupendous Mountain," where he came into the Bella Coola Valley. The country crossed by Mackenzie is depicted on the modern chart in this way: there is a plateau (tinted yellow on the chart, but, in reality, green with trees) of about forty-five hundred feet in elevation and about 150 miles across; then the Coast Mountains, and beyond them an archipelago of mountainous islands off the Pacific coast.

The West Road River was not navigable by Mackenzie's twenty-five foot canoe, and from its mouth on the Fraser River Mackenzie walked overland, going west-southwest, parallel to the West Road River. Mackenzie, who had lost his compass in the Peace River, noted on July 11, 1793: "As I had hitherto regulated our course by the sun, I could not form an accurate judgment of this route, as we had not been favoured with a sight of it during the day."

I followed Mackenzie up the West Road River, which flows 135 miles down from the forested plateau. This river (also called Blackwater) is not much bigger than a creek, which in its lower course runs through gorges and boasts rapids and waterfalls. In many places, the river appears to be quite impassible, which is why Mackenzie and his party had, by this point, cached their canoe and proceeded on foot.

I climbed to eight hundred feet above the ground, to see ahead. On this clear day, I could see the snow-capped Coast Mountains on the horizon. From the ground, however, folds in the foothills would probably obscure these distant peaks much of the time, though Mackenzie several times mentioned the mountain views. He first noted them when about halfway up the West Road River: "We now discovered the tops of mountains, covered with snow, over very high intermediate land."

The West Road River next passes through a chain of lakes, which made map reading relatively easy. The lakes (Kluskoil, Euchiniko, and Tsacha) showed up well from the air, whereas the narrow river runs through forests and it was not easily visible to me.

I was flying over a wilderness, inaccessible except on foot or by floats. The route that Mackenzie "discovered" was an Indian "grease trail," a trade route for taking the congealed oil of the eulachon fish inland. Because of its difficulty, the route is impractical for modern commerce, and no paved road or railroad follows it today. Bella Coola is served by a secondary highway from the town of Williams Lake, on the Fraser River, but that road is seventy miles south of Mackenzie's track.

Along Mackenzie's track, there were signs of logging, a few hunting lodges and seaplanes, and then, beyond Tsacha Lake, some outback ranches with zigzag fences. Above them, an eagle circled at my altitude, eight hundred feet above the ground. I took it as a good omen.

Routinely, I looked for forced landing places. Now and then one of these elderly aero-engines will fail—a broken exhaust valve, or, more rarely, a failed crankshaft; sometimes, water in the fuel. More usually, the plane runs out of gas because the pilot got lost or neglected to top up the tanks.

Against these contingencies, the pilot in the North is required to carry survival equipment. The trouble is that staying alive in the wilderness might require special skills, too—skills that a lot of us don't have. To make up for this lack of knowledge, I carry in my kit *Herter's Professional Guide's Handbook*. Its topics include:

Catching trout with your hands.
The correct method to make and set snares.
Using a horse to get into gun range of geese and ducks.
How to make spears if lost.
Getting out of quicksand, bog, or mire.
What to do in an avalanche.
How to enjoy eating raw meat.

My main fear is the mosquito. I imagine these insects crawling over every square inch of my face, neck, and hands. I packed a bug jacket in the back pocket of my lifejacket, along with a couple of containers of concentrated insect repellant. If I go down in the bush—and I can fend off the mosquitoes—I figure that, somehow, everything else will get

worked out. But if I should go down, I will try to set down on water, where I can be spotted. Going down in the bush, even in Virginia, is a sure-fire way to disappear for months—and out here, forever.

Beyond the headwaters of the West Road River, several more lakes helped blaze the trail until I came to a pair of lakes, called Tanya Lakes. Here, the route enters the foothills of the Coast Mountains, rugged country with the sharp white peaks of the main range beyond.

To fill in the gaps for this segment of Mackenzie's journey, I took along a trail guide, which I'd had the luck to pick up during my stop at Old Fort William.

MacKenzie's party supposedly went around the east flank of what is now called Mount Mackenzie. But the aeronautical chart seems to represent, with tinted contours, a valley aligned north-south on the west flank of Mount Mackenzie, butted against the Bella Coola valley. This, I thought, would be the best route for a low-flying plane.

As it turned out, my "valley" was so inconsiderable when seen from the air that it might as well have been nonexistant. (The only obvious route to the sea was the Dean River Valley, just to the north. Why didn't Mackenzie's Indian guides take him that way? Bands of the Bella Coola Indians lived on the Dean River as well as in the Bella Coola Valley, to the south.)

I was now flying south at five hundred feet above the ground—five thousand feet above sea level—and could not see the pass at the end of the valley that was marked on the half-million scale chart. I made a climbing 360 degree turn to gain another two thousand feet, and re-oriented myself with Tanya Lakes, back there over my left shoulder.

My objective, the Bella Coola River valley, remained hidden, just as it had to Mackenzie. The fact that I had wider views than Mackenzie hadn't helped me. I'd as soon have hiked over the alpine meadows of Mackenzie's route, maybe seen a wolf or a bear.

According to the trail guide, "Mackenzie's exact route off the 2000 metre alpine slopes to the Bella Coola Valley is a matter of conjecture." Following my version of his route, I flew south towards a col, or small gap (you could not call it a pass). Then there appeared, right on the seaplane's nose, an impressive mountain.

> Before us appeared a stupendous mountain, whose snow-clad summit was lost in the clouds; between it and our immediate course, flowed the river to which we were going. (Mackenzie, *Voyages*.)

Giving the col the benefit of the doubt, I scribbled in my flight log, "scary pass." Immediately over the col, with the "stupendous mountain" in my windshield confirming that I was close to Mackenzie's track, I looked to the right and saw the wide glen of the Bella Coola River going twenty miles down to an arm of the sea: a splendid avenue to the Pacific.

* * *

Mackenzie's Indian guide, having marked the way by breaking the branches of trees, preceeded him into a village at the foot of the mountain. When Mackenzie and his party arrived,

> [My host] directed a mat to be placed before me and Mr. Mackay, [then] he brought a salmon for each of us, and half an one to each of my men.

Next day, after a breakfast of "some berries and roasted salmon," Mackenzie and his party hitched a ride down river, in two dugout canoes, to the next village.

🛶 Thursday July 18, 1793. . . . At one in the afternoon we embarked . . . in two canoes, accompanied by seven of the natives. The stream was rapid and ran upwards of six miles an hour. I had imagined that the Canadians who accompanied me were the most expert canoe-men in the world, but they are very inferior to these people, as they themselves acknowledged. . .

When we came in sight of the village, we saw them running from house to house, some armed with bows and arrows, others with spears, and many with axes, as if in a state of great alarm. . . . I had but one line of conduct to pursue, which was to walk resolutely up to them. . . This . . . produced the desired effect, for . . . the greater part of the people laid down their weapons.

The conduct of the Indians then progressed through curiosity to hospitality, and:

🛶 Soon after I retired to rest that night, the chief paid me a visit to insist on my going to his bed-companion, and taking my place himself; but notwithstanding his repeated entreaties, I resisted this offer of his hospitality.

The next day, Friday, Mackenzie persuaded the chief of this village to take his party by canoe to Bella Coola.

🛶 Saturday July 20, 1793. We obtained a larger canoe . . . and . . . at about eight [A.M.] we got out of the river, which discharges itself by various channels into an arm of the sea. The tide was out. . . . The surrounding hills were involved in fog. I had flattered myself with the hope of getting a distance of the moon and stars, but the continually cloudy weather disappointed me, and I began to fear that I should fail in this important object. (Mackenzie, *Voyages*.)

Mackenzie's Track · 139

And this was all he had to say about the climactic moment of reaching the Pacific. He was "all business," choosing to ignore both the drama of the moment (no great shout, as reported by Xenophon of his men at the end of their long march); and the poetic possibilities exploited by Keats ("He stared at the Pacific—and all his men/Looked at each other with a wild surmise").

Mackenzie was preoccupied with confirming his position.

As I could not ascertain the distance from the open sea, and being uncertain whether we were in a bay or among inlets and channels of islands, I confined my search to a proper place for taking an observation. (Mackenzie, *Voyages*.)

On July 21, 1793, Mackenzie and his party canoed along the as yet unnamed fiords on the coast until they reached a defensive spot on the other side of Dean Channel from what would be called King Island, near Cascade Inlet. This place is called "Mackenzie's Rock."

We were soon followed by ten canoes. . . . From their general deportment I was very apprehensive that some hostile design was meditated against us, and for the first time I acknowledged my apprehensions to my people. . . . We took possession of a rock, where there was not space for more than twice our number, and which admitted of defending ourselves with advantage, in case we should be attacked. (Mackenzie, *Voyages*.)

The following morning, Mackenzie inscribed on the rock, in vermilion mixed with grease, that famous inscription: "Alexander Mackenzie, from Canada, by land, twenty-second of July, one thousand seven hundred and ninety-three."

* * *

In the valley of the Bella Coola, flying west in the still air, below the level of the surrounding peaks, I began to feel complacent. I had stuck on Mackenzie's trail and was about to close in on him. Freed from the chore of closely reading the chart—the Pacific Ocean was visible, at the end of the glen—I relaxed, and speculated about the distance to China.

Below me was a small land airport, supposedly equipped with a "remote communications outlet"; I decided to indulge in a call on the radio. Normally, I dislike talking in the air. It breaks the spell of flight. But now there seemed some magic in a "wireless" call to a hearer on Vancouver Island, distant I didn't know how many capes and promontories. I called out my position. To my surprise, I was instantly answered by a cheerful voice. "Do you still plan on Bella Bella?"

"Yes," I answered.

I passed over the little town of Bella Coola and along the pale turquoise fiord called North Bentinck Arm, which is walled in by snow-capped mountains. I was on my way to Mackenzie's Rock. By coincidence (for I am hopelessly behind schedule), this is July 21st—the very day that Mackenzie had canoed along these waters.

I would finally catch up with him. I'd looked for Mackenzie among the high-rise buildings of Montreal, almost caught up with him on the shore of Lake Superior, lost the trail at Frog Portage, then glimpsed his canoe beneath the white pelicans soaring over Manitoba. I couldn't find him at Fort Chip, lost the trail again at Crooked River, but picked it up and followed him to the Stupendous Mountain. Now I'd catch up with him in Dean Channel.

To find my way through the fiords to Dean Channel, I merely had to take the third turn to the left. This I did—I thought I did—following the route with my finger on the chart. But when I didn't see Cascade Inlet, a prominent perpendicular feeder fiord, I realized that I was on the wrong side of King Island—the near side. I had taken the second left turn, not the third. I was flying down a channel, Burke Channel, that Mackenzie described, as he passed it by, as "about two miles and a half wide at South-South-West and [I] had a view of ten or twelve miles into it."

I was flying about three thousand feet lower than the mountains on both sides, so I climbed up to fly through a pass across King Island (so named by George Vancouver, who had mapped the area only seven weeks before Mackenzie arrived in these waters). Once through the pass, I turned southwest down the correct fiord, Dean Channel. But I had missed Mackenzie's Rock, just as Mackenzie had missed Vancouver.

I did not trust my navigation enough to search for it. The route had looked obvious enough when I was sitting in the hotel last night, looking at the chart. But the real world of low flying in the mountains is not the flatland of a chart, but a very different land of vertical perspectives. I turned towards a town on the shore of Dean Channel to orient myself. I couldn't place the town on the chart, and when I got nearer I saw that the "town" was a collection of felled trees. Then I looked west, and fifteen miles away, off the coast, I saw a place that could only be Bella Bella, shining in the sun.

* * *

Bella Bella is the nearest suitable seaplane base on this coast. It is a scattered settlement, consisting mainly of a town, Waglisla, which is ninety percent Indian and situated on Campbell Island, and a place called Shearwater, on adjoining Denny Island. Once a Hudson's Bay post (they were everywhere, from the Arctic to the Pacific), Bella Bella had re-established itself with a Japanese shellfish cannery at the turn of the century; Shearwater owed its rebirth to a 1940 airbase. The major industry now is fishing, with some lumbering.

The fishery works twelve months a year, packing salmon, cod, or herring, according to the season. There are several fish packing plants at Shearwater, and a shipyard able to haul boats out of the water for repair. A surprising number of the fishing boats are of wooden construction, at least fifty years old. One such, with her bow stove in below the water line, was under repair while I was at Shearwater. Her captain was not a happy man—he would miss the salmon season.

Of the three seaplane landing areas shown at Bella Bella, Shearwater is the most convenient for me because it has a hotel here with a seaplane dock handy. Fuel, however, has to be obtained at a different dock.

* * *

I arrived from Bella Coola at 1:00 P.M., and circled the harbor at Shearwater. I picked out a landing path that would avoid floating logs strewn about the harbor waters, then landed and taxied up to the jetty, and called to some fishermen to take my strut. They were glad to do so, but said I was at the wrong place. The seaplane dock was over there, they said, pointing to a vacant dock in the corner of the harbor.

"Where are you from?"

"Montreal."

"Hey, this guy came all the way from Montreal! In a little plane like that!"

It was my moment of triumph, diluted somewhat by my botching the approach to the dock they had pointed out. I cut the engine too soon and the seaplane drifted away from the dock before I could jump ashore. I restarted the engine and succeeded in getting ashore on the second attempt.

It is the snuggest little harbor yet, a floating dock attached by a hinged walkway to accomodate the tides, which here average eight to twelve feet, but can go as high as seventeen feet. (For comparison, the tidal range at Baltimore is about two feet.)

"Watch the ravens don't steal your rubber float plugs," a bystander said. I secured the plane to the dock and walked over to the hotel, which faces the water front only two hundred yards from my plane.

This evening I saw a fog bank, very solid, very white, lying on the water. "You'll get fog from now 'til September," I was told.

"Better get yourself a radar reflector," another chipped in. "Last year we were sailing along in dense flog when we saw a radar blip ahead. It turned out to be a floatplane sitting on the water. There were two tenderfoots aboard. They were lost." Then he added, "I don't know what sort of a map you have."

Monday July 22, 1793. The Indians were still threatening and Mackenzie's men urged him to leave. But Mackenzie wished to take advantage of the clear day to establish his position.

🛶 My people were panic-struck, and some of them asked if it was my determination to remain there to be sacrificed? (Mackenzie, *Voyages*.)

After Mackenzie had inscribed his "brief memorial" on the rock, he consented to move three miles farther on, away from the village of hostile Indians; he then resumed his observations, and left the place at "ten o'clock in the afternoon."

🛶 I had now determined my [latitude and longitude], which is the most fortunate circumstance of my long, painful, and perilous journey, as a few cloudy days would have prevented it. (Mackenzie, *Voyages*.)

Like Mackenzie, I have achieved my objective of reaching the Pacific, and am ready to turn around and go back East.

"We're supposed to be in New York next week," said Carolyn, on the telephone. "Why don't you just leave the plane where you are? I'm afraid you'll kill yourself otherwise."

🛶 The voyage was openly execrated. . . I assured them that as my particular object had been accomplished, I had now no other but . . . safety. (Mackenzie, *Voyages*)

Days 27–30

✈ *Day Twenty-Seven*

Sunday July 22, 1990. There is no way I can be in New York by August 1st. Not unless I take the jetliner from Seattle. I decided to go to Seattle today.

5:30 A.M. Fog. Visibility 200 yards.
6:00 A.M. Fog has lifted somewhat—I can see the island a quarter of a mile away. Wind intermittently flutters boat pennants in the harbor.
9:30 A.M. First glimpse of sun.
11:30 A.M. Clear. A low-flying eagle flaps laboriously around the harbor while a second eagle, higher up, circles effortlessly in a thermal.

The weatherman briefed me over the telephone. "There is fog all around Vancouver Island. It looks like it will clear up, but it's difficult to forecast around there. It will probably clear around two o'clock, but north Vancouver Island may have fog patches throughout the day. You should be able to make it through. You'll see the mountain ranges sticking out of the fog to give you bearings and it's clear halfway down the strait."

"I'm not familiar with this coast and I have no radio aids. I need to see the coastline."

"Yeah, you might turn down the wrong inlet. Call me back. The weather could change."

At 2:00 P.M. I called back. The weather, said the man at

Port Hardy (a place right there, in the strait), had deteriorated, perhaps temporarily. I called the seaplane base at Sullivan Bay, which is on the other side of the strait from Port Hardy, to get their weather report, but there was no answer. I decided to give the flight a try, anyway. I checked out of the hotel, and went to the dock. Someone there told me, "The marine forecast predicts fog coming in early." I looked seaward and saw low stratus clouds that might cut off my retreat; I was spooked out of going.

This evening, back in the hotel, I studied the chart and wondered if I should have gone. It had been clear halfway down the strait. I would only have had to keep the mountains of the mainland on my left until I picked up landmarks in the Strait of Georgia. It would have been easy had I had a radio direction finder to home in on one of the stations on Vancouver Island.

"Fog is holding me on the coast," I reported to Carolyn.

Staying in this hotel are two salmon-spotter pilots and a logger. (The wife of the logger, a cheerful man of only medium size, works at the hotel.) He is from Edinburgh, Scotland, he says, and he is a small-time contractor, who logs areas on the coast unprofitable to the big companies. He and his crew stay out a few weeks at a time, living on a barge off the shore they are logging. (This smiling man, then, is the much-advertised, grinning arborcide of the Tourist Board.)

"I won't pick up a saw for less than three hundred dollars a day," he said, knowing his worth.

Well, I thought, here's this lone, smallish logger, more potent than a score of conservationists. While they're in a policy meeting, he'll cut down a thousand-year old tree.

These are fine, free-wheeling folk, these despoilers of nature. Certainly as congenial as the yachting family from Seattle—pleasant folk, not free-wheeling—who confided, in rather a hurt way, "This place is a dump." They sailed in looking for some Carmel-by-the-Sea, and were disappointed with the workaday place they'd found. I didn't know what to say. I haven't seen any boutiques, either.

July 23, 1793. Mackenzie's party returned to the mouth of the Bella Coola River ("The only bird we saw today was the white-headed eagle"), and encountered more harassment from the Indians, at "Rascal's Village" (a name politely omitted from the Trail Guide).

Day Twenty-Eight

July 23, 1990. Around 10:00 A.M., before the fog had lifted at Bella Bella, I called Port Hardy. I got another equivocal weather report and forecast. After reeling off the lighthouse observations, the weatherman said, "It looks pretty good. Of course, we don't get observations between the lighthouses, so it could be zero-zero in places. There's a lot of moisture about."

"Better give it a try, or you may be here 'til September," said Carl, the fish-spotter pilot.

About noon, the fog lifted to form low clouds. I checked out of the hotel and took off at 12:15 P.M. I flew over Fitzhugh Sound past hundreds of salmon boats. I flew at three hundred feet over the water, under the low stratus clouds. I was near enough to the fishing boats to watch the one-man skiffs stroke out, then drag the purse seine nets in a circle back to their mother ships, where the nets were pulled in with their harvest of salmon.

I could see about ten miles ahead. Just below me, the Pacific swells crashed against the rocky coast. "Why am I doing this?" I wondered.

The Lycoming kept pulling. Conditions at the Egg Island Lighthouse were still good, but somewhere short of the Pine

Island Lighthouse, at the head of Queen Charlotte Sound (not far from where Vancouver's ship, *Discovery,* had run aground) I turned back—I couldn't see half a mile ahead. I landed back at Shearwater after two hours in the air.

Later, one of the fish-spotter pilots—experienced local pilots who habitually fly in poor weather—reported that it had cleared again at the top of the Sound. But there is no place to set down and wait off that coast. One must go on or turn back.

"I'm going to try to get to Vancouver overland," I said.

"Don't do it," said Carl. "I've known too many who didn't make it through those passes."

A Note on Fog: Vancouver's first attempt, in August 1792, to survey the entrances to Fitzhugh and Queen Charlotte Sounds was marred by extensive fog. When he returned in May 1793, he was able to detect numerous errors in the earlier survey, which "on this occasion were in some degree corrected."

A Note on Salmon: Carl says there are now one thousand fishing boats within sixty miles of Bella Bella.

Of the abundance of salmon hereabouts, Vancouver noted, on June 28, 1793, that the Bella Bella Indians presented one of his survey parties with two fine salmon, "each weighing about 70 lbs."

Day Twenty-Nine

July 24, 1793. Mackenzie's party, their goal accomplished, spent the day going back up the Bella Coola River. During the ride up the river, in rough water, the natives "almost filled the canoe with water, by way of a sportive alarm to us."

July 24, 1990. I, too, hoped to be on my way. But it rained

heavily all morning and into the afternoon. Flying for me was washed out for the day. I needed to top up the engine sump with oil, though, as I had been unable to purchase any at my last two stops. Between rain showers, I topped up the oil level from stored drums at the marina. It was awkward work. The oil cap was on the off-side of the engine from the dock, and I could only get to the far float by holding onto the propeller and walking along the quarter-inch cable that Ed Kelly had stretched between the bow cleats of the two floats.

As I was pouring the last third of a container of oil into the engine, I noticed that it poured rather too quickly. It did not have the viscosity of normal oil and I suspected that water had got into the drums. I put a plank between the floats, and placed on it another borrowed can, just below the engine drain. When I released the drain valve, a stream of clear water poured out of the sump and into the can. By the look of things, most of the water had already settled on the bottom of the engine sump and had now drained out. Just to be sure, I drained all the engine oil and replaced it with fresh oil that I obtained from Carl, the fish-spotter pilot, who has access to a cache around the point.

Before yesterday's flight, I topped up the oil in my plane from the same bad drums at the marina. That lot must have been free of water, or the engine would have seized in flight.

At 3:00 P.M. Carl returned from a flight and said, unexpectedly, "It's clear down the strait."

I didn't even check out of the hotel this time, just grabbed my things, refuelled the plane and, at 4:00 P.M., took off from Shearwater harbor.

I flew away under the low stratus clouds and headed south down the coast again towards the strait, past the tree-clad mountainsides that looked so much like the West Indies—but the trees were conifers, not palms.

I passed Egg Island Lighthouse at 4:48 P.M., flying under grey skies and looking down again on the great swells of the

Pacific. I crossed the strait and arrived over Port Hardy, on Vancouver Island, at 5:10 P.M. I radioed the flight service station there, and asked about the weather at Campbell River, 120 miles farther on. The operator said, "Standby," and, after maybe a minute, reported that the visibility at Campbell River was fifteen miles. I went on.

All along Vancouver Island, along Johnstone Strait, were the bare hillsides and the ugly debris of logging. I was witness to an event of sorts: the end of the old forest at which Mackenzie had marvelled.

July 25, 1793. . . . [There was] the finest wood of cedar trees that I had ever seen. I measured several of them that were twenty-four feet in the girth, and of a proportionate height. The alder trees are also of an uncommon size; several of them were seven feet in circumference, and rose to forty feet without a branch; but my men declared that they had, in their progress, seen much larger of both kinds. (Mackenzie, *Voyages*.)

Half way down Vancouver Island I came to the dangerous-looking swirls in Discovery Passage, the narrowest part of the strait, where the tides and current may attain fifteen knots. (Vancouver's two ships, the *Discovery* and the *Chatham*, passed northward along this strait in July 1792.)

I landed here at Campbell River at 6:30 P.M. What a relief! Yet was an easy-enough flight.

Day Thirty

July 25, 1990. (The seaplane base at Campbell River is remarkable for the number of eagles that roost there.)

I had not planned for my re-entry into the United States and, after a number of telephone calls to U.S. Customs, I found that I wasn't allowed to go to Seattle because of my limited radio equipment. I decided to go to Bellingham. I was advised to clear customs and immigration at San Juan Island, a U.S. outpost located just east of the city of Victoria.

I took off from the tiny Campbell River and flew down the strait, farther down the east shore of Vancouver Island, until I reached San Juan Island. There I circled over congested Friday Harbor where I was reminded, by the intense activity below, that there are twenty million pleasure boats in North America, but only seven thousand seaplanes. There was one seaplane amidst all the boats and I landed in the boat swell near the seaplane and taxied up to the dock. The pilot of this seaplane told me I was at the wrong place and directed me to the busy marina in front of the town. I made a lengthy taxi across the water in amongst the boats and the ferries and eventually found a section of the marina with a sign, "Seaplane Dock." I recalled the intimacy of a very different arrival in Quebec at the beginning of my flight: two small figures awaiting me on a lonely dock on the St. Francis River.

The Return

At length, as we rounded a point, and came in view of the Fort, we threw out a flag, and accompanied it with a general discharge of firearms. . . . Here my voyages of discovery terminate. (Mackenzie, *Voyages*.)

*M*ackenzie's party re-crossed the mountains, found their canoe where they had left it, and returned down the Peace to Fort Chipewyan, where they arrived, September 10, 1793, eleven months after they left.

I left my plane at Lake Whatcom, near the city of Bellingham, where it was subsequently sold. The following day I rode a jetliner from Seattle back East, to Washington D.C., where Carolyn was waiting for me. The flight took four hours and twenty-eight minutes.

I spent that brief time, inside the closed metal cigar-tube body of the jetliner, reflecting on my trip. First, what would Mackenzie have thought of it? Surely he would be surprised to know that a man could, in four short weeks, fly a small seaplane along the rivers and lakes that he, Mackenzie, knew so well, travelling with ease along a route that had taken his utmost fortitude to complete. But it was not something he would have done himself, I decided. Alexander Mackenzie was not the sort of man to travel for recreation.

As for me, I was already experiencing a letdown from the daily high of getting up not knowing the day's outcome. That particular high was over for a while.

P · A · R · T III

Particulars

Why did it take three hundred years to cross North America? What happened to the fur trade; and to the Indian tribes encountered by Mackenzie? Why did Mackenzie rely on Galileo's method for determining longitude rather than on the newly-perfected chronometer? These and other inquiries spilled over into some supplementary chapters—an update of sorts to Mackenzie's own book.

Tethered to bank with ground anchors. Tabor Lake, B.C. July 20, 1990. Floatplanes are best operated from sheltered lakes like this, not large areas of water like Lake Winnipeg, or fast-flowing rivers like the Fraser.

The Crossing of North America

🛶 June 29, 1793. . . . an observed immersion of Jupiter's first satellite made our longitude 122.48. West of Greenwich. (Mackenzie, *Voyages*)

*I*n 1763, the year the French ceded Canada, and almost two hundred fifty years after Magellan circumnavigated the globe, a significant portion of the earth's surface remained unknown and unmapped. Not only had many places never been visited, but the instruments with which to map and survey them had hardly been perfected. A map of inland North America, in 1763, was a fair representation of the eastern third of the country, so far as it went; but it went no farther than Lake of the Woods. Beyond that were "Parts Undiscovered."

Peter Pond's map, drawn in 1787, placed Fort Chipewyan only 150 miles from the Pacific Coast. The coast was placed more or less correctly on his map because it was based on information from Captain Cook's voyage of 1778. But Pond, not knowing how to determine longitude, had mistakenly—and optimistically—displaced all the lakes and rivers west of Lake Superior farther to the west, so that Fort Chipewyan, on his map, was located at longitude 130 Degrees West. Hence, Pond and the younger Mackenzie, who were both based at Fort Chipewyan in the winter of 1787–8, believed that the Pacific Ocean was only a short distance away. In 1788, however, a Hudson's Bay Company surveyor commissioned by the British Government determined the location of Fort

Chipewyan to be 110 Degrees 30 Minutes West, and it became clear that reaching the Pacific Ocean overland remained a formidable task.

In the account of his first voyage of discovery, by canoe to the Arctic Sea, Mackenzie determined the longitude of only one position—the mouth of the Mackenzie River, at 135 Degrees West—and that subsequent to the voyage, by dead reckoning. (His dead reckoning was not far off, because of his carefully kept log of compass courses and distances run, and his use of an azimuth to periodically check magnetic variation.) Mackenzie was not a surveyor; he did not undertake mapping as such. He plotted his course by compass, estimated his distance run—he doesn't mention towing a log—and carefully established his latitude by sextant at key points along his route.

When Mackenzie went to London at the end of 1791 to acquire navigation instruments and to learn the techniques of their use, he must have been primarily concerned with the problem of longitude. He would also have seen the latest maps of the Pacific coast of North America, although there was nothing really new, for current information was based largely upon Captain Cook's cruise up the coast in 1778 in search of a Northwest Passage. There were also miscellaneous reports from trading ships; Mackenzie refers in his book to Captains Meares and Gray. Gray discovered the mouth of the Columbia River, but this information was not available to Mackenzie in 1792 when he set out on his trip to the Pacific. When Mackenzie set out from Fort Chipewyan, the coast, though cruised by Cook and by navigators of other nations, was unsurveyed, and the maps, sketchy. The only permanent European settlement north of California was a Russian post near present-day Kodiak.

The problem of determining longitude by a practical method, though, had been solved, thanks in large part to Sir Cloudsley Shovell, who ran his fleet aground on the Scilly

Isles in 1707. He was reinterred in Westminster Abbey beneath a handsome and rather absurd memorial by Inigo Jones that depicts the deceased sailor (attired in Roman toga and sandals, and a flowing Restoration wig) in a nonchalant pose, reclining full length on his tomb, leaning on one elbow, and with an expression that seems to say, "Well, really, you didn't expect me to concern myself with petty details like longitude."

Parliament, who had to pick up the tab for sunken naval ships, offered a handsome prize for an accurate method of determining longitude, and the prize was eventually won by John Harrison for his chronometer. The principle was this: if a navigator had an accurate timepiece set to Greenwich time, and he knew the local time (from observation of the sun at noon), then his longitude was the time difference, in hours from local time, divided by fifteen (since fifteen degrees equals one hour, and 360 degrees equals twenty-four hours). Harrison's chronometer proved its accuracy on a 1761 voyage to Jamaica, by producing a longitude error of only one mile. Cook carried a Harrison chronometer on his second and third voyages (1772–75 and 1776–79 respectively).

Why did Mackenzie prefer Galileo's old, "fussy," method of determining longitude over the chronometer? At least four possibilities come to mind:

1. First-class chronometers (as distinct from deck watches) were expensive and difficult to obtain.
2. A fine chronometer would not stand up to the rough usage it would get in the course of a long canoe trip.
3. Chronometers needed to be "rated" by astronomical observations. (Vancouver, who was equipped with five of the best chronometers in the world, found that all, to varying extents, gained time.) Why not use astronomical observation as the primary method?
4. Although Galileo's method was useless at sea, on a pitching deck, it was workable on land (Mackenzie may have

seen the method used when the longitude of Fort Chipewyan was determined in 1788) and tolerably accurate. When Mackenzie had ample time for observations, he determined his longitude with an accuracy of within five to ten miles.

Mackenzie's book was published at the end of 1801, and much had happened in the interval since the completion of his expedition to the Pacific. In April 1791, Cook's former lieutenant, Captain George Vancouver, left England to survey the Pacific coast of North America. He completed this task with great diligence, returning to England in October, 1794. (When "Macubah," as the Indians called him, mapped Dean Channel on June 3, 1793, he missed Mackenzie by only seven weeks). The results of his voyage, together with relevant charts, were published in 1798 in his book, *Voyage of Discovery to the North Pacific Ocean and Round the World*. This work was available to Mackenzie when he was finishing his own account.

In recording his movements on the coast, Mackenzie followed his usual procedure of listing courses and distances travelled. He also confirmed his positions, in three footnotes, by reference to Vancouver's survey. Mackenzie's book included a map by Arrowsmith, the London map maker. Looking at this map of North America, one is struck by how Vancouver's detailed survey "anchored" Mackenzie's single probe to the Pacific coast, and nicely complemented the plotted track of the overland journey. It occurred to me that Mackenzie delayed his book to await Vancouver's findings. Yet we may take Mackenzie's explanation for the delay at face value.

The delay actually arose from the very active and busy mode of life in which I was engaged since the voyages have been completed; and when, at length, the opportunity arrived, the apprehension of presenting myself to the Public in the character of an Author, for which the course and

TABLE 1. Positions as Determined by Mackenzie

Location	Per Mackenzie	Actual	Notes
Winter camp at Peace & Smoky rivers, 6 mls. beyond fork	117.35.15 W 56. 9 N	117.28 W 56.9 N	(1) longitude ascertained by observations of Jupiter on several occasions. (2) long. error—about 5 st. mls. to West.
Peace River Canyon, at Portage Mountain	120.29.30 W 56.0. 47 N	122.13 W* 55.58 N	(1) observation of Jupiter's second satellite, 5/22/93. (2) long. error—67 miles to East
Arctic Lake (source of Parsnip River)	121 W 54.24 N	121.41 W 54.25 N	(1) longitude determined by dead reckoning 6/12/93 (2) error—about 28 mls East
On Fraser River, at Canoe Island, 1-1/2 days paddling south of mouth of West-road River	122.48 W 53.3.7 N	122.33 W 53.05 N*	(1) observations of J's first satellite 6/29/93 (2) about 11 miles West of actual position
Mackenzie's Rock, in Dean Channel (latitude only)	52.21.33 N 52.20.48 N	52.22.30 N*	(1) Mackenzie's two latitudes taken by artificial and natural horizons, respectively
Dean Channel, 3 mls. NE of Mackenzie's Rock (longitude only)	128.2 W	127.26 W*	(2) longitude determined by observations of J's first & third satellites, 7/22/93 (3) about 25 miles West error

* From Lamb

occupations of my life have by no means qualified me, made me hesitate in committing my papers to the Press. . . (Mackenzie, *Voyages.*)

Mackenzie's explanation was to be mirrored by Thomas Jefferson's lament (to von Humboldt), more than six years after the return of the Lewis and Clark expedition, that ". . . the death of Capt. Lewis, the distance and occupations of General Clark, and the bankruptcy of their bookseller, have retarded the publication." Besides, we can easily accept Mackenzie's idea of authoring as a major undertaking in that day—it was the age of Boswell, Gibbon, and Burke; and more particularly of the accounts of the voyages of Cook and Vancouver.

It is also possible to speculate that Mackenzie's disappointment at not finding a practical trade route on either of his long trips to the sea may have influenced him to think that his accounts did not merit publishing. Besides, compared to the practitioners in the Royal Navy, Mackenzie must have recognized that he was an amateur navigator. It was five years before he took credit for reaching the Arctic Ocean and proving that "a North West Passage is impracticable," and he explained to the Governor of Canada that, "Not having been furnished with proper Instruments to ascertain the Longitude in my first Expedition, I made myself but little known during my residence in London the Winter 1791/2. . . ."

Perhaps it was only gradually that he realized he could turn failure into glory. By his trip to the Arctic Sea he had disproved the existence of a Northwest Passage; by his trip to the Pacific Ocean he had become the first man to cross continental North American (even if his claim to have proved "the practicality of a commercial communication between the Atlantic and Pacific Oceans" is arguable). Like Lindbergh, he was to gain fame in his time not so much for doing anything directly useful, but rather for doing it with flair and exciting his age to commercial possibilities.

Mackenzie's journey to the Arctic Sea confirmed that there was no practicable Northwest Passage around North America; the ocean was frozen. Mackenzie did not find a corresponding navigable route across North America—there isn't one. Later, another Northwester, David Thompson, managed to portage from the Saskatchewan to the Columbia River, reaching its mouth on July 15, 1811. But this was not a practical route either. It might be argued that the first and only navigable route across—or around—North America was via the Panama Canal. Hence it was Balboa who actually discovered the ultimate route, in 1513.

Mackenzie himself, in the conclusion to his book, advanced the argument that the most logical navigable route across North America would be from Hudson Bay to the Columbia River, and he lobbied, unsuccessfully, for British Government financing to improve that route.

In his day, Mackenzie fairly claimed that his work "extends the boundaries of geographic science, and adds new countries to the realms of . . . commerce." Today, a traveller across Canada can only be astonished at his achievement in crossing the vast and inhospitable northern lands in a flimsy bark canoe.

But why was Mackenzie the first to cross continental North America? Why did it take so long from the day in 1535, when Jacques Cartier climbed Mont Royal to look westward to the Pacific? Or from 1579, when Francis Drake visited for a month on the California Coast?

The answer probably lies in the fact that every overland attempt (up to the Lewis and Clark expedition, in 1804–6) had to be a self-financing venture. The European governments, who were well capable of financing the crossing of North America, were not interested; they even discouraged exploration.

Unlike Spanish America, with its gold and silver mines, North America wasn't considered particularly valuable. Extensive lands, of themselves, didn't seem that important to European governments. In 1680, for example, the exports of the tiny island of Barbados were more valuable than the entire exports of North America. European governments did finance numerous expeditions to go around North America by a "Northwest Passage," whose supposed attractions did not wane until the nineteenth century. From Columbus on, a westward route to the Orient was the goal, to obtain the riches described by Marco Polo.

If anything, the search for the Northwest Passage may have delayed the finding of an overland passage across North America. (The energy and cost expended on the hundred Arctic expeditions would have sufficed to have crossed North America overland many times. The Grail-chasing explorers—they provide a curious counterpoint to the practical frontiersmen and settlers who simultaneously colonized North America—pursued the delusion of a Northwest Passage for three hundred years.

A predecessor to Mackenzie in an overland search for the Pacific was Samuel Hearne. Hearne was only twenty-five when he started out on his long walk north from Churchill in 1771, looking for fabled copper mines, and the Northwest Passage besides. Accompanied only by an Indian guide and the guide's eight wives, Hearne journeyed for eighteen months, through country that wouldn't be revisited by white men until the 1920's.

Hearne and Mackenzie demonstrated that there was no Northwest Passage aside from the totally impractical Arctic Coast route. But the search for this Holy Grail went on until the loss of Sir John Franklin and his expedition in 1847.

Mackenzie's employers were interested in exploration only to the extent that it was profitable. In 1784, the directors of the North West Company wrote the Governor-in-Chief of Canada that they had in view exploring, at their own expense, a route to the Pacific. They asked, unsuccessfully, for ten years exclusive rights to the route they might discover. Mackenzie's two trips, though tolerated by his employers, were considered by them a commercial failure. By then, though, the idea of crossing the continent, instead of going around it by a Northwest Passage, had gathered enough momentum that Mackenzie gained considerable fame for being the first man to cross North America.

Even so, the modern idea of being first to do something for its own sake (first up Everest, or first to canoe across the Atlantic) had hardly caught on. It is, after all, a sophisticated—even frivolous—idea. It didn't enter the Spaniards' heads. To such men—"men on the make"—being first was only worthwhile if it resulted in a claim to wealth. Balboa crossed to the Pacific Coast because the Indians, presumably referring to the Inca Empire, told him that that was where the gold was. Balboa did receive some temporary favor for his discovery, but the Spaniards were not much kinder to each other than they were to the Indians, and he was soon beheaded at the order of a jealous rival.

Another gold-seeking Spaniard, Nuñez Cabez de Vaca, came near to crossing the continent without meaning to. He was one of four survivors of a party of four hundred that set out from the Gulf Coast of Florida, looking for El Dorado, and was picked up eight years later wandering near the Gulf of California.

That Alexander Mackenzie was the first across the continent was due to the circumstances of the fur trade and to the personality of Mackenzie himself. Mackenzie was a man of enormous energy, and he had the intellect to direct his energy, and the self control to achieve his ends.

Mackenzie was what we now call "an achiever." Born in the Outer Hebrides of Scotland, in 1763 or '64, he emigrated to New York as a youngster, moved on to Canada, apprenticed as a clerk to the fur trade at the age of fifteen, became a partner in the profitable North West Company at twenty-three, discovered a route to the Arctic at age twenty-five and, in 1793, at age twenty-nine, became the first man to cross the continent north of Mexico.

Of all Mackenzie's qualities, the ability to lead men was probably the most important. He had no other means, other than his natural decisiveness, than persuasion to keep his men from turning back, something they often felt impelled to do. Whereas Lewis and Clark could, and did, order fifty lashes for absence from camp, seventy-five lashes for "mutinous expression," and one hundred lashes for drunkenness, Mackenzie could only appeal to his men, flatter them, ridicule them sometimes, reason with them, and encourage them to "forget their fatigues and apprehensions."

From the U.S., by Land

Thomas Jefferson, who had nursed the idea of a transcontinental expedition for twenty years, took the opportunity to implement the scheme immediately after the Louisiana Purchase. He was much interested in Mackenzie's book, which proved useful in planning the Lewis and Clark expedition. The two expeditions can be said to have been complementary, not duplicative. Their *modus operandi,* though, was similar; the Lewis and Clark expedition of 1804–1806 was a larger and slower version of Mackenzie's trip of 1792–1793.

Both were conceived as waterborne expeditions, which would leave a jumping-off place (both fur-collecting centers as it happened—St. Louis, Fort Chipewyan), and go up river (Missouri, Peace) to the respective headwaters, from where they hoped to "carry over" to a west-flowing river (Columbia, "River of the West").

TABLE 2. Comparison of Mackenzie and
Lewis & Clark Expeditions

Mackenzie		Lewis & Clark	
Leaves Fort Chipewyan	10/10/92	Leave St. Louis	5/14/04
Along Peace River to winter camp, arrives	11/1/93	Along Missouri to winter camp, arrive	10/26/04
Leaves winter camp	5/9/93	Leave winter camp	4/7/05
Gateway to Rockies (on Peace)	5/31/93	Gateway to Rockies (on Missouri)	7/19/05
Reaches headwaters of Peace	6/12/93	Reach headwaters of Missouri	8/10/05
Crosses Divide	6/12/93	Cross Divide	9/19/05
Finds west-flowing river	7/3/93	Find west-flowing river	9/22/05
Reaches Pacific Ocean	7/20/93	Reach Pacific Ocean	11/15/05

Neither expedition expected to reach the Pacific in one season, and both made winter camps (Fort Mandan, Peace River). Both entered the Rocky Mountains through spectacular gorges (Gates of the Mountains, Forks of the Peace).

Both expeditions encountered their greatest problems in finding a way from the headwaters of the east-flowing tributary (Jefferson, Parsnip) across to west-flowing streams (Clearwater-Snake, Fraser-West Road River). This difficult task took Lewis and Clark eight weeks; Mackenzie, over three weeks.

Both expeditions had to cache their canoes and travel overland for a period. Both had to build new canoes. Both suffered from hostile Indians, lack of supplies, and rugged terrain.

Both depended on the Indians for guidance and forbearance.

The effects of Mackenzie's and Lewis and Clark's expeditions were similar. They showed the way to opening up much of the interior of North America, a result applauded by all except crusty Thoreau, who cared not for "the Mississippi or the Pacific, nor conduct toward a worn-out China and Japan." In Thoreau's view, all of America would go the way of the Maine woods.

> Think how stood the white pine tree on the shore of Chesuncoock, its branches soughing with the four winds, and every individual needle trembling in the sun light,—think how it stands with it now,—sold perchance to the New England Friction Match Company! (*The Maine Woods*)

Four generations after Thoreau, and four thousand miles west of Maine, the loggers were clearing the offshore islands on the Pacific Coast. It is an interval of time and distance nicely bridged by the progress of the extractive industries, by the fur and the logging industries in particular.

Following Captain Cook's cruise along the North Pacific coast in 1778—and his report on the abundance of sea otters—British trading ships began to arrive on the coast in numbers, mostly for the purpose of procuring sea-otter pelts for the China trade.

One such was the ship *Queen Charlotte,* which in 1787 was the first to trade with the Haida Indians on the islands now known as the Queen Charlotte's, whose southern tip is one hundred fifty miles west of Bella Bella. The bicentenary of this ill-omened contact was marked by a minor, but significant, furor when the remnants of the Haidas objected to the lumber industry's insistence on removing the last old-growth cedars from the Islands, from tiny off-shore Lyell Island. Even while a national park was debated, "The spring logging crews ripped through Lyell Island with unprecedented speed." They were only following a tried-and-true method: work the vein until it is exhausted.

Modern Canoe Crossings

🛶 . . . [we] arrived at [Fort Chipewyan] on the 29 September, which was our fifty second day from Lac La Pluie [Rainy Lake], and the shortest voyage I believe that has been performed to this quarter with laded canoes. (*Alexander Mackenzie to the North West Company, February 15, 1789*)

*I*n an attempt to put Mackenzie's crossing in better perspective, I read the accounts of several modern trans-Canada canoe trips. They confirm the almost superhuman effort required to go "coast to coast."

New York to Nome: The Northwest Passage by Canoe tells the story (fifty years after the fact) of two young men, Taylor and Pope, who made that trip in 1936–7, before all the dams, when the country probably hadn't changed much since Mackenzie's day. Port Arthur (now part of Thunder Bay) was "almost a town." The Pas was "a quaint settlement of rustic cabins," and Fort McMurray was "one muddy main street, with cabins strewn across an open flat."

The first season's journey was from New York City's 42nd Street to Fort Smith, on the Slave River. (In the second season they completed the expedition to Nome, 7,165 miles from New York.) From Lachine to Fort Chipewyan, they followed the voyageurs' route, taking 144 days, May 13, 1936 to about October 3, the same year. Though they pushed themselves to the limit, their pace seems to have been slower than the pace of the voyageurs.

The leader of this expedition, Shell Taylor, upon whose recollections the account is based, seems to have been, by his own admission, pretty much insufferable. Was it his pushiness, his bumptious vitality, that enabled him to set such a goal and carry it through? Certainly Taylor was of that school who meet obstacles aggressively.

It worked. He scoffed at problems. Of the terrors of the Winnipeg River: "I could hardly keep from laughing"; Of the Manitau Rapids on Rainy River: "Like so many times before, we found the locals overestimated what they had." He got into a fist fight with his partner.

What luxury for me to go solo, in a seaplane.

Where Rivers Run is a slower-paced account of the same extra-normal activity, long distance paddling. In this instance, it was a six thousand-mile canoe trip that the author, Joannie McGuffin, and her husband took in 1983–4, from Baie Comeau, near the mouth of the St. Lawrence River, to the Beaufort Sea. (They broke their journey at The Pas, and wintered at home.)

Canadian in temperament (reserved—dull, almost, as contrasted with the pushier American), it is an account of the country as the McGuffins saw it in 1983–4. It had changed since 1936; and changed since Eric Morse wrote, "These routes in the nineteen-sixties remain dramatically unchanged from what the first fur-seekers saw three centuries ago."

Morse's "beautiful canoeing" route—the route I had followed, during a brilliant day, along the shore of Lake Huron to the Soo, and around Lake Superior's shores—was much degraded when seen from McGuffin's canoe. The clear lakes I had seen along the shore of Georgian Bay were dead from the effects of acid rain. The MacGuffins encountered a bad chemical spill off Thessalon, behind Manitoulin Island, and "a poisonous stream of effluent" from the pulp-and-paper mill at

Marathon, on the north shore of Superior. And there was more pollution to come, along the Winnipeg River.

We get two for one in McGuffin's book. It is a commentary on the despoliation of the country, as well as the record of an arduous trip. (Before making their canoe journey, the energetic pair hiked the entire length of the Appalachian trail; subsequent to the canoe trip, they undertook a seventy-five hundred mile bicycle ride.)

Magnetic North: A Trek across Canada from the Pacific to the Atlantic by Foot, Dogsled and Canoe is the account of the late David Halsey, a young American who lived near me in Virginia, though I didn't know him. He accomplished his feat in 1977–9, with one partner, Peter Souchuk. In the course of this punishing forty-seven hundred mile trek, they canoed along the Athabasca, Berens, Albany, Rupert, and several other rivers, as well as around the south end of James Bay. Halsey's account vividly describes the unpleasantries encountered:

> Along one particularly grueling stretch we climbed up and over twenty-four falls and rapids in two twelve-hour days. At many of these the only portage trail was that of the old freight brigades, now lost under fifty years' growth.

Elsewhere, Halsey says:

> After a particularly rough set of rapids, we would shake from nerves and have to take a ten-minute break to calm ourselves before running the next.

Like the other two books, *Magnetic North* is a story of endurance, but it goes further than that, to the point of mortifying the flesh.

What these undertakings had in common with each other—and to some extent with my seaplane trip—is their hurry. Canadian distances and the Canadian climate do not favor lollygagging about. Thoreau, a sometime paddler on the Penobscot River, could afford to disdain "days . . . minced into hours and fretted by the ticking of a clock." But he didn't attempt a transcontinental canoe outing.

What these undertakings had in common—but not with my seaplane flight—was uncommon physical exertion. I enjoy reading about long canoe trips. For long-distance water journeys, though, a float plane suits me just fine. Come to think of it, Mackenzie wasn't an eager paddler, either. He mostly left that necessary chore to his voyageurs, "whose strength is lost in premature old age."

The Survival of the Beaver Hat

*M*ackenzie was a fur trader, and his continental crossing can hardly be understood outside the context of the beaver-felt hat, and the highly profitable trade resulting from the long term popularity of that headgear.

Beaver fur was essential to high-quality men's hats from the fourteenth century to the mid-nineteenth century, and even into the present. In the earlier period, the fur came from Russia and the Baltic, and from 1600 on, from North America. Samuel Pepys, the diarist, noted on June 27, 1661, that he acquired "a bever, which cost me 4£ 5s." (It was more than the annual salary that he paid his "Cooke-maid.")

The hat industry was for many years the largest consumer of furs, particularly of beaver fur, from which was made the best felt. (The Hat Act of 1732, though, restricted the North American hat trade in favor of English manufacture.) The best felt hats were always made entirely of fur. The traditional beaver hat was made of felted rabbit fur with a beaver felt nap added as a second step in the manufacture.

The kinds of felt hats fashionable during Mackenzie's time were the wide-brimmed top hat and the more informal lower-crowned, wider-brimmed hat. The cocked hat of George Washington's day was on its way out.

Whatever its style, the beaver hat was a well-made, durable thing. ". . . hard and heavy. It sounded upon an entrance-hall table like a drum." So durable were these hats that there was a large second and third-hand trade to Spain, Brazil and Africa.

About the time the umbrella became popular, the beaver-felt hat was replaced by the silk top hat, and eventually by a dozen other, less formal hat styles. But the hat, as such, remained indispensable until the mid-twentieth century, long after the beaver hat had had its day. Early twentieth-century photographs of crowd scenes—greeting Lindbergh in Paris, volunteering for the Great War—show a sea of hats; so, too, movies of the 1930's and 1940's.

Today, the hat is almost superfluous, and its indispensability in the past—and the incredible expenditure of energy in paddling canoes thousands of miles to procure beaver fur to make felt for hats—seems strange if not downright absurd. ("There is always something absurd about the past," said a wit.)

Today, in North America, the home of casual wear, the ordinary man's—Joe Sixpack's—everyday hat of choice is overwhelmingly the baseball cap, a form of head gear worn in one of four ways: outdoors—worn fore-and-aft; in-doors (the hat is rarely removed)—tilted back on the head; passive-aggressive mode—worn back to front; and counter-culture—beak to the side.

It was cold in Montreal, and I bought such a cap. I wore mine fore-and-aft. I lost it in North Bay, and bought a replacement there—with the letter "B" on the front. This was undoubtedly meant to be "Boston," though the hat was made in Taiwan.

Except in deepest winter Pepys's twentieth-century descendant, buttoned-down man, disdains headgear. It was the often-bare-headed Prince of Wales, in the 1920's, who first challenged the dominance of the conventional felt hat; it finally fell almost entirely out of fashion after 1960, the year John Kennedy, who rarely wore a hat, became President of the United States.

That's good enough for a hatter's history of Europe and

most of North America. ("As far as Boston goes," a westerner told me, "and all those Eastern cities for that matter—Baltimore, Phillie—if you've seen one, you've seen 'em all.")

The Western perspective I got from Mr. H. T. King. I met Mr. King one morning when I happened to accompany Carolyn to Triple R Western Wear in Falls Church, Virginia. After I'd occupied myself by looking at the framed photographs of B-Western Stars in the entrance, I picked up a cowboy hat and looked inside and read "Stetson Hat Co. 4 X Beaver." A real beaver hat? They still make beaver hats? I would ask about this. The proprietor, H. T. King, an old timer in a string tie, turned out to be more interested in singing cowboys. "I see you were looking at my pictures," said Mr. King.

Back in the 1940's, B-Western stars—their well-known sidekicks, anyway—spent a lot of time on the road, trading on their screen image, entertaining the folks in towns throughout the continent. It was during this time, when H. T. King managed two movie theaters in the Shenandoah Valley, that he got to see a lot of Hollywood in the flesh.

According to King, the biggest money-making western stars in those days were Gene Autry and Roy Rogers. They both worked for Republic Pictures. Republic brought in Roy because they didn't want all their eggs in one basket—Gene was getting difficult about his rate of pay.

Back when Roy was with a singing group called Sons of the Pioneers (and singing songs like "Tumbling Tumbleweed," and "The Last Round-Up") his name was Leonard Slye, and he wore "the biggest black hat in the world." One day in 1937 he took his Stetson into a hat shop in Glendale to have it reblocked. There he heard that Republic Pictures would audition for singing cowboys the very next day. He went to Republic's studios next day, producer Sol Siegel auditioned him, and he was hired. Then Sol and his brother Moe decided that Leonard Slye was not such a great name for a movie actor, so

Leonard got the name Roy Rogers. And he took to wearing a white Stetson hat, as befitted the new King of the Cowboys.

Gene Autry and Roy Rogers didn't appear in the Shenandoah, but a lot of the also-rans did. They would spend a couple of nights in town, and they invariably brought a horse and a band.

"What if they couldn't sing?" I asked H. T. King.

"Why, they just stood and twirled their pistols—or did lariat tricks—while the band played on."

The Stetson hat is made in St. Joseph, Missouri, where the West begins, where Mark Twain bought a $150 ticket on the overland stage to Carson City.

John B. Stetson started making beaver-felt hats about the time Mark Twain went out West, though the company didn't move from "Phillie" to Saint Joe until later. Among Stetson's first models was "Boss of the Plains,"—what a grand name—a ten-gallon hat with a high, rounded top and a broad brim.

Stetson's factory in Saint Joe is only the final stage of manufacture. Beaver and rabbit pelts are received at Newark, New Jersey, from Canada and Australia respectively, and the fur shorn off and bagged. Next, the fur is sent to the felting plant in Longview, Texas, where it is cleaned and mixed and formed into thirty-inch-tall cones of loose fur—the first shape of the hat body, just as it looked two hundred years ago. Between seven and eight ounces of mixed fur goes into today's low-crowned Stetson hat. The tall-crowned nineteenth-century beaver felt hat took nine to twelve ounces of beaver fur in addition to rabbit fur. Because of its two layers of felt, it shed water better than today's beaver hat.

After forming the cones, felting proper beings. The process of felting has remained essentially unchanged for hundreds of years, and consists of applying heat, moisture and mechanical action to the loosely formed cones of fur in order to interlock the fibers and produce a non-woven fabric—felt. The cone is shrunk in hot water, pressure rolled, shrunk and rolled again, dyed, shrunk and rolled again, and shellacked. The tip of the cone is stretched and rounded, and a rim is shaped. Then it is shipped to Saint Joe, where the hat is blocked into final shape and size, finished and trimmed with sweat band and lining. (By now the hat has been handled forty-three times.) Stetson sells seven grades of hats, designated 4 X to 30 X (the higher grades have a greater proportion of beaver fur). In 1991 they introduced a 100 X hat; it is a mixture of beaver fur and cashmere, and it retails for one thousand dollars. Not expensive for a good hat, eh, Mr. Pepys?

The Fur Trade: On the Skids

🛶 The fur trade, from the earliest settlement of Canada, was considered of the first importance to that colony. (Mackenzie, *Voyages*.)

After the fashion of his day, Mackenzie gave his book a long and comprehensive title that concluded "with an account of the rise and state of the fur trade." It takes very little space to bring that account up to date here.

In Mackenzie's day, the fur trade generated, in his own words, "profits surpassing anything in America." Today, it is all but dead, a casualty of falling demand for furs.

The fur-bearing animals are still there, though. The 1986/7 figures (before the slump in demand for furs) suggest good remaining populations of fur-bearing animals. Mackenzie's tally of pelts, sold by the North West Company in the year 1798, included 106,000 beaver, 32,000 marten, and 17,000 muskrat. The 1986/7 figures (for wildlife pelts taken in the whole of Canada) were 500,000, 222,674, and 1,700,000 respectively. The number of beaver taken was unchanged from 1980/1.

Two hundred years has seen a lot of change. After a period of ferocious competition, which Mackenzie helped foment, when the sales of the North West Company were several times greater than the Hudson's Bay Company, the latter company absorbed the newer North West Co. in 1821. There had been constant friction between the two companies, not least over the question of whether the North West Company infringed on the monopoly of the Hudson's Bay Company to trade in the lands that drained into Hudson Bay. (The North West Company claimed it had inherited the old French rights to trade up the St. Lawrence and into the *pays d'en haut*.) After the merger between the two companies, furs were no longer shipped through Montreal, but travelled the shorter route to London through Churchill.

The heyday of the voyageur had passed; the lines of communicaiton were much shorter, and the annual exchange of furs and trade goods at Fort William was no longer necessary. The terms of trade to the Indians did not improve, though. John Bigsby, a traveller in Canada at the time, noted that a handkerchief that sold for a shilling in England cost twenty-five shillings in Indian country.

The demand for felt hats (and therefore beaver pelts) eventually fell off, offset by the demand for fur clothing. What did not change was the atavistic desire to be clothed in fur. In the 1930's and 40's, every European and American woman wanted a fox pelt (with grinning mask) draped around her neck; Amelia Earhart wore one. In the 1980's, every prosperous German businessman, it seemed—a horde of otherwise respectable Huns—must be seen arriving at his office (in the winter) in a fur coat.

In 1970, the headquarters of the Hudson's Bay Company moved from London, England, to Winnipeg, Canada. In 1987, the Company, strapped for cash because of rapid expansion in the big cities, sold off its 187 northern stores. By the time of my tour through Canada, the Hudson's Bay sign had been taken down from the northern stores. Too bad.

Hudson Bay itself, the inland sea that provided the short route to England and enabled the Bay Company to undersell the Montreal-based North West Company, had not been used, I was told, for the past three years, and the port of Churchill had been idle (because the Europeans no longer bought Canadian grain). The fur trade only limped along, for the campaign by conservationists against perceived cruelty to animals has been very effective.

Appendices

Flight of Seaplane N72475 Distances & Times* To:

		St. Mls.	Hrs
0	Back River (Baltimore): Starting Point	—	—
1	Connecticut River (East Haddam)	365	3.5
2	St. Francis River (Drummondville, Que.)	385	3.7
3	Trout Lake (North Bay, Ontario)	395	4.5
4	Wa Wa Lake (Ontario)	370	4.0
5	Lake Superior (Thunder Bay, Ont.)	240	3.0
6	Lake of the Woods (Kenora, Ont.)	340	3.8
7	Icelandic River (Riverton, Manitoba)	170	2.0
8	Grace Lake (The Pas, Man.)	330	4.0
9	Lac La Ronge (Saskatchewan)	260	3.0
10	Churchill Lake (Buffalo Narrows, Sask.)	150	2.0
11	Small Lake (Fort Chipewyan, Sask.)	300	3.7
12	Footner Lake (High Level, Alberta)	250	3.0
13	Charlie Lake (Fort St John, B.C.)	385	3.7
14	Tabor Lake (Prince George, B.C.)	325	3.4
15	Pacific Ocean (Bella Bella, B.C.)	350	3.7
—	Bella Bella & return	—	2.1
16	Campbell River (B.C.)	235	2.5
17	Friday Harbor (San Juan Is., USA)	150	1.6
18	Lake Whatcom (Bellingham, Washington)	35	0.6
	Totals	5,035	57.8

* includes time on water

Equipment Carried

They are then dispatched from La Chine, with eight or ten men in each canoe, and their baggage; and sixty-five packages of goods, six hundred weight of biscuit, two hundred weight of pork, three bushels of pease, for the men's provision; two oil cloths to cover the goods, a sail, etc., an axe, a towing-line, a kettle, and a sponge to bail out the water, with a quantity of gum, bark, and watape [thread made of the split roots of the black spruce], to repair the vessel. (Mackenzie, *Voyages*.)

*F*or my flight across Canada I carried, in addition to Mackenzie's book, the following:

a complete set of charts
300′ of mooring lines
a transceiver radio with headset
a mooring bridle for the propeller
7 lb Danforth anchor
ground anchors
1 gall. lead dispersant
a siphon pump
a fuel/filter funnel
an oil funnel
a 5-gall. gas can
a tool kit
a float repair kit
a life jacket

In compliance with Canadian regulations for flight over the Sparsely Settled Areas, I carried:

Equipment Carried · 187

a tent
a sleeping bag
a long-handled axe
a saw
a trowel
a cook pot
a bug jacket
insect repellant
rations for two weeks
fishing lines
a first-aid kit
other items, n.e.c., contained in a commercially produced "Two-man Survival Pack."

Contrary to Canadian regulations, I did not carry a rifle, as I could not find a light-weight model.

With extra fuel, my plane was overloaded about 120 lbs. and, like Mackenzie's canoe, was "laden, heaped up, and sunk with her gunwhale within six inches of the water."

Postscripts

[I was] secure in the belief that Canada, at least, is too big to be entirely trashed.

1. *The Churchill River.* By 1976, engineers had diverted much of the flow of the Churchill River into the Nelson. It was the first large river diversion and lake impoundment in widespread permafrost. Rising water on the Nelson has melted the permafrost and destabilized the shoreline; nesting waterfowl have disappeared, and mercury is being leached out of the rocks and poisoning the fish. More megaprojects are planned in Manitoba, Quebec and British Columbia (at Kemano, north of Bella Coola). Summarized from "Dammed and Diverted," by Larry Krotz, *Canadian Geographic,* Feb.–Mar. 1991.

2. *The Boreal Forest.* The Alberta Government has leased more than one quarter of the province to a dozen—mostly foreign-owned—giant pulp firms for clear-cut forest projects, mainly on the Athabasca and Peace rivers. The Alberta-Pacific mill alone would discharge more than seventy-seven million litres of toxic effluent per day into the Athabasca River. Summarized from "Pulp from the North. Alberta's plans to clear-cut its boreal forest," by Des Kennedy. *Canadian Geographic,* June–July 1990.

3. *Vancouver Island.* There remain five last watersheds (out of one hundred) on the west shore of Vancouver Island that have escaped logging. The tallest tree in Canada grows here, a

Sitka spruce 312 feet tall, discovered by a logging engineer in June 1988, in the Carmanah Valley. Townspeople in nearby Port Alberni want more logging in Carmanah Valley, not less. These giant conifers are doomed to disappear, after covering the northern Pacific coast since the last Ice Age fourteen thousand years ago. Summarized from "New Bird in a Battered Forest," by Erich Hoyt and Susan Milius. *International Wildlife,* March–April 1991.

The French & the Indians since Mackenzie's Time

*E*ven in Fort Chipewyan, you can't get away from the news. And it's news with a different focus, hard for an outsider to understand. In 1990, Canadian television and newspapers were full of the French and the Indians. A stranger, a traveller such as myself, is left to make what sense out of it he can.

> Saying they are tired of being humiliated and betrayed by their English conquerors, the Quebec Tories . . . join a pro-sovereignty movement. . . "Since the Royal Proclamation of 1763, the goal of our new conquerors was to assimilate us." (The Montreal *Gazette,* June 27, 1990)

What is this all about? About events long-dead, yet unburied, I suppose. The explanations lie moldering in the history of the French in America, and of their Indian foes and allies. If one had time and inclination, he might look them up, I suppose, in the seven volumes of Francis Parkman's life work, *France and England in North America.*

Set in the "pristine barbarism of the North American forests," this history tells how Champlain paddled up the Richlieu River, in 1609, with a party of painted Hurons, whom he helped to defeat the Mohawks. The history concludes with the year 1763, with the Treaty of Paris, which settled the Seven Years War, and incidentally, the French and Indian War. Included in its terms was the cession of Canada, and its sixty thousand French-speakers, by France to Great Britain.

Today, as I had seen, two hundred thirty years later, the six million descendents of the sixty thousand French speakers of 1763 drive around with their car licence plates proclaiming, "*Je me souviens.*" ("I remember")

Ignoring the Indians' own remembrances, the mayor of an obscure Quebec town named Oka, on the Ottawa River, decided in June, 1990, to extend the municipal *club de golfe* by nine holes—right over an old Indian burial ground. There ensued an armed confrontation, in which a policeman was killed, and Indian protests spread through Quebec and the rest of Canada.

A group of Mohawks from the Kahnawake reserve just south of Montreal turned commuter traffic to chaos late Wednesday when they blocked the Mercier bridge leading to Montreal. They were acting in sympathy with the Mohawks at nearby Oka, who were fighting police over the expansion of a golf course. (*Newspaper Report,* July 12, 1990)

Meanwhile, other Indians, nationwide, had been activated by the fracas at Oka.

Chilcotin Indians threaten blockade
B.C. band may cut off logging
to force land claim settlement

The natives say clear-cut logging and the extensive logging-road system have devastated the game population and trap lines the Chilcotins followed in their traditional migratory lifestyle for 5,000 years.

"A very few militant native Indians have chosen to draw an area on the map the size of many European countries and proclaim it as theirs," Mr. Richmond, the Forests Minister, said. (*Newspaper Report,* July 2, 1990)

Just as the French-Canadians see 1763 as the crucial date in their history, so do the Indians see their loss of independence as dating from the treaties they signed—or didn't sign—with the white man. The treaties are apparently not comprehensive or watertight, since there are continual attempts to re-interpret them. I was told that the Indians in British Columbia—where few treaties were negotiated—claim one hundred fifteen percent of the province.

Mackenzie's Indians

What became of the Indian tribes encountered by Mackenzie in his journey west to the Pacific? *The Indians of Canada,* a publication of the National Museum of Canada, has this to say:

The Cree, hunters and trappers, ranged a large territory from what is now the Province of Quebec west to Lake Winnipeg. They were once an aggressive tribe, but epidemics of smallpox (1780, 1838) and the effects of TB and influenza, typhus and alcohol, ruined them. They are still, though, the largest of the Indian tribes.

Chipewyan: these edge-of-the-woods hunters controlled a vast area in the boreal zone. Less numerous than the Cree (they may have numbered only 3,500 in pre-European times) they suffered similar effects to the Cree from contact with the white man.

Beaver: these hunters, who occupied a territory west from Fort Chipewyan, were reduced in numbers, by 1924, to about six hundred.

Sekani: the "people of the rocks" (Rocky Mountains) were hunters who controlled the basins of the Parsnip and Finlay rivers, and the valley of the Peace half way to Lake Athabasca. Their pre-European population may have exceeded one thousand. By 1923, they numbered 160, plus some Métis.

The Carrier were fish-eaters, who lived in the valleys of the Upper Fraser and Blackwater rivers. "The name refers to their peculiar custom of compelling widows to carry on their backs the charred bones of their dead husbands." Because of an abundant food supply, they were relatively numerous, 8,500 in 1780, but declined to about two thousand in 1932.

The Bella Coola, salmon eaters, occupied as many as forty villages on the Dean and Bella Coola rivers and on the fiords into which these rivers flow. The population in 1793 (the year of Mackenzie's visit) may have been three thousand, of whom thirty percent could have been slaves. By 1932, the total population was reduced to three hundred, all in one village at the mouth of the Bella Coola River.

The original population of aboriginal Indians in British America, that is to say Canada, is estimated to have been 221,000. (*Enc. Brit.* 13, 215.) The *Canada Yearbook* for 1990 reports that in 1986, the number of "single origin" North American Indians was 286,230. About 400,000 more persons were counted as "multiple origin," with Indian blood.

Despite the heavy losses to disease following their contact with the white man—nine-tenths of the Chipewyans are reported to have died of smallpox in 1781—the Indians have increased their numbers.

On a canoe trip along the Churchill River in 1960, Sigurd Olson remarked on the number of Indians he saw, "certainly more than could live off the country." The Indians had clearly recovered from the toll taken by the white man's diseases. (There were no overt wars against the Canadian Indians: most of their lands were not tillable, and the Indians themselves were needed as fur trappers.)

The apparent inconsistency of the Indians' increase in numbers in spite of the calamities that befell them, can largely be explained by a very high birth rate in the 1950's and 1960's—a phenomenon assisted by the benefits of Canada's welfare state.

Despite high government expenditures, the lot of the Canadian Indian is not an enviable one.

> Life expectancy [of the Indian] is about ten years less than the average in Canada. Infant mortality rates are double, and accidents and violence—involving motor vehicles, fires, drowning and suicide—are a major cause of death for native Canadians. Between 1984 and 1988, accidents and violence accounted for a third of all Indian deaths (four times the rate in the general population). (Montreal *Gazette*, June 27, 1990.)

Some of the Indians blame this on the second great disruption of their life style (the first being the coming of the white man): the phenomenon of moving to town.

> Presently, nobody lives in the bush. They are all in town. They lost their independence, self respect, and self esteem . . . about 75% turned to drinking and doing drugs to fill in the boredom they faced. (Therese Tuccaro, of the Cree Band. *Proceedings,* Fort Chipewyan Bicentenial Conference, 1988.)

N · O · T · E · S

THE CANOE AND THE PONTOON

p. xvi The thirty-six foot fur-trade canoe weighed six hundred pounds empty, and was paddled by about ten men. It was used on the broad waterways from Montreal to Superior. The Northwest canoe was twenty-five feet long and weighed three hundred pounds.

p. xvi There are three types of seaplanes: the pontoon-equipped aircraft (the floatplane); the flying boat, which lands on its hull, rather than on pontoons; and the amphibian, which is a floatplane or flying boat with wheels attached.

p. xvii The construction of the bark canoe is described in the definitive book, *The Bark Canoes and Skin Boats of North America*, by Adney and Chapelle.

WATERBORNE

p. 7 . . . air rudder will oppose water rudder . . . When drifting backwards, the wind strikes the air rudder from the front, but the relative motion of the water against the water rudder is from astern. Hence, the water rudder must be retracted when drifting backwards.

p. 11 The Lycoming 0-290. According to Jane's *All The World's Aircraft*, 1942 edition, the engine's bore and stroke are $4\frac{7}{8}$ in. × $3\frac{7}{8}$ in.

p. 10 The seaplane rating check is conducted by an examiner designated by the Federal Aviation Administration.

WHICH WAY TO THE COAST?

p. 16 "in his spare time . . ." Mackenzie's trip to the Pacific, like his trip to the Arctic, "was as much or more Mackenzie's own

195

project as it was the company's." (*Lamb, p. 14*.). As a partner in the business, Mackenzie seems to have had considerable independence of action.

p. 17 "Morse does not deal with Mackenzie's route to the Pacific. . ." I used Woodworth's *Trail Guide* for the last 250 miles to the ocean, but had no backup to Mackenzie's own account for the stretch between Lake Athabasca and the Fraser River, hence some difficulties later on, along the Parsnip. (Unfortunately, I did not at that time have the Hakluyt edition of Mackenzie's *Journals*.)

p. 19 Pond's Map is reproduced in *The Canadians* (Time-Life Books), and in the Hakluyt edition of Mackenzie's *Journals*.

p. 19 "broad river avenue to the Pacific." The Columbia River was unknown to Mackenzie at the time of his trip.

p. 20 Alexander Mackay was to be killed a few years later, in 1811, along with the crew of the American ship *Tonquin*, by Indian attack, on Vancouver Island.

p. 20 Distance. Surprisingly—because Mackenzie was meticulous in recording his day-to-day progress—his narratives do not specify the overall distances travelled by him to either the Arctic or Pacific oceans (although many intermediate distances are given). I mentioned this fact to Messrs. Ince and Baldwin, staff members of the National Maritime Museum at Greenwich, England, and they showed me a hand-written note by Mackenzie that addressed the point:

> Athabasca is 2750 Miles to the North and West of Montreal . . . I . . . passed on to the Peace River in which I went about 450 Miles against the Current to . . . where I passed the winter. [From there] it took me 30 days to get to the Source of the River distance about 400 Miles. . . . We carried our Canoe and Lading over [the] portage went with the Current [and got] to a Larger River . . . going down it about 420 Miles. . . . I returned some distance up the River left my'Canoe in Latitude 53 north Longitude 122. 43 West from this in 17 days I got to the Sea Coast our Course about West and distance 250 Miles.

(This note, I later found, is reproduced in the Hakluyt Society's edition of Mackenzie's *Journals*.)

Mackenzie underestimated the distances to Athabasca, and to the source of the Peace, and his estimate of 420 miles down a "Larger River" (his diversion down the Fraser) is not very helpful in reconstructing the mileage travelled across the continent. Not finding a convincing estimate for Mackenzie's mileage travelled, I added up the numbers myself:

3,000 miles from Montreal to Fort Chipewyan (*by measurement, on a quarter-million scale map*—this confirms Morse's figure);

1,090 miles along the Peace River to the source of its tributary, the Parsnip, at Arctic Lake (*from the Gazetteer*);

170 miles from Arctic Lake to the mouth of the West Road River, net of his diversion down the Fraser, (*by measurement,* on a 1:50,000 scale chart).

220 miles overland to the Bella Coola River, and 35 miles down that river (*Woodworth*);

40 miles to Dean Channel, where he took his definitive position.

p. 21 Speed of canoe. Mackenzie's "shortest voyage"—fifty-two days from Rainy Lake to Fort Chipewyan—was achieved at an average speed of thirty-two miles per day (including portaging). Under the most favorable conditions, a canoe could travel sixty miles in a day.

BEHIND THE EIGHT BALL

p. 25 Lack of directional stability of the floatplane. . . To correct this, some floatplanes are equipped with auxiliary fins. (Canoes also suffer from a form of directional instability when paddling across the wind—the canoe wants to swing farther off the wind, and it may require two paddlers to stroke on the same side to keep a straight course.)

p. 31 Landing on the grass. If handled expertly, a floatplane can land without damage on a grass surface. It needs a dolly to take off again.

DAY TWO

p. 43 Voyageurs' Church. . . I later read that the modern church I saw at Ste. Anne de Bellevue was built on the foundations of the voyageurs' church.

p. 46 Two of Mackenzie's crew accompanied him on both his great expeditions. They were Joseph Landry and Charles Ducette.

DAY THREE

p. 49 Extent of pine forest. And, Thoreau reminds us, it included "The greater part of New Brunswick, the northern half of Maine . . . not to mention the northeast part of New York."

p. 49 The Premier of Canada. Laurier, Sir Wilfred. "The Forests of Canada." *National Geographic*, September 1906. Farmers made it a practice in the eastern woodland to finance their land clearing by burning the woods to produce potash, the only forest product (between the end of the Napoleonic Wars and the onset of the railway boom) to justify the freight to Britain.

DAY SIX

p. 57 Newspaper report. I retain the clipping, but did not note its source.

p. 58 The correct techniques for taking off in confined waters are explained in *How to Fly Floats,* and other books. (See listing)

THE CANADIAN SHIELD

p. 70 The Soul of Canada. Catalogue. *The Canadian Landscape.* An exhibition of paintings, 1915–1939. Jeremy Adamson, Guest Curator. Canadian Embassy, Washington D.C., 1990. (The exhibition featured "The "Group of Seven," of whom A. Y. Jackson may be best known.)

p. 71 Sigurd Olson. His books include *The Lonely Land,* an account of a canoe trip from Île-a-la Crosse to Cumberland House; and *The Singing Wilderness,* about the Quetico-Superior country, a place he helped protect from roads, resorts, dams, logging—and floatplanes.

DAY ELEVEN

p. 77 The dispatcher. In most air taxi operations, there is a sort of duty officer who schedules flights, and keeps track of the weather.

p. 77 Claude Dablon and the Japan Sea. Quote is from Lavender, *Winner Take All*.

DAY FIFTEEN

p. 85 "an organized lot. . ." It was not always so. "At the time when the white men contacted the Indians, social structure tended to be extremely simple. The Indians had . . . no special officers charged with the task of coordinating groups." *Enc. Brit.* 1, 694, "American Sub-Arctic Cultures."

p. 86 "scalped. . ." But the haircut grew out well.

DAY SIXTEEN

p. 89 Cumberland House: "Miserable site." Ref., Lavender. *Winner Take All*. CH was one of three main provisioning depots for the North West Co. The other two were at Bas de la Riviere (at the mouth of the Winnipeg River) and at Île-a-la-Crosse.

p. 89 Squaw Rapids Dam is west of Cumberland House, about sixty miles up the Saskatchewan River.

DAY TWENTY

p. 104 Peter Pond. Description is from Bigsby, *Shoe and Canoe*.

DAY TWENTY-ONE

p. 107 Lake Athabasca. In Mackenzie's time, it was called Lake of the Hills and is named as such in the maps reproduced in Mackenzie's book.

p. 109 Mackenzie's editor was William Combe. He worked on Mackenzie's journals while in debtors' prison. Combe had already edited Captain John Meares' *Voyages* (London, 1790).

DAY TWENTY-FOUR

p. 118 Wood buffalo. Most of these were to be killed in 1991 because they harbor TB and brucellosis, diseases transmitted to them by domestic cattle.

p. 120 Fort Vermilion. This is the northernmost significant area of farming in Canada. It is often referred to as prairie, though it is cleared forest.

p. 120 The town of High Level is on the Mackenzie Highway, which goes north to the Great Slave Lake.

DAY TWENTY-FIVE

p. 121 "Wop" May. Canada has a tradition of independent and aggressive fliers. Of the top seven British air aces of World War One, four were Canadians. Notable were Lt. Col. Bishop (from Ontario), 72 victories; and Maj. Barker (from Manitoba), 53 victories.

p. 121 Death of Von Richthofen. Australian ground fire may have killed the Red Baron, but the air force confirmed Brown's claim to the kill.

p. 121 The story of the gold prospector comes from *The Challenge of the Skies* (Edmonton: Pukrin's Production House, Ltd., 1981)

p. 121 Canada's air transport system in the 1920's. See: Wilson, "Gentlemen Adventurers of the Air." *National Geographic,* November 1929. The photographs illustrating this article are of great interest.

p. 122 Jupiter's satellites. *Enc. Brit.* 6. 190. "Eclipse, Occultation, and Transit."

p. 122 Establishing position. An alternative method to Galileo's was the measurement of lunar distances, developed in the 1770's. It was used by Vancouver, Lewis and Clark, and occasionally by Mackenzie himself (January 10 and July 20, 1793). The angular distance between the moon and the sun, or the moon and one of the fixed stars, was determined by observation, and the time when the observation was made was compared with the time at which the same lunar distance would have been observed at Greenwich. These Greenwich observations were published in the *Nautical Almanac*.

p. 124 Rapids below Bennett Dam are in the Peace Canyon, just below the dam. Completion of this dam, in 1969, diminished the ferocity of these rapids.

p. 124 ". . . where I wished to fall upon the Pacific Ocean. . ." Mackenzie evidently still hoped to get to Cook Inlet and the northern coast where the Russian otter and sealing grounds were.

p. 128 Down the Crooked River. In an article, "Across Canada by Mackenzie's Track," in the *National Geographic,* August 1955, author Ralph Gray wrote that Mackenzie had made a misjudgement by not following the Pack and Crooked rivers. I read this after I had written my own account. The Pack River is pretty small, and Mackenzie showed a certain logic in staying with the Parsnip. From the air, though, even at low altitude, it seemed obvious to follow the Pack-Crooked rivers rather than follow the Parsnip into the mountains. Simon Fraser also criticized Mackenzie for not following the Pack River.

DAY TWENTY-SIX

p. 132 The country Mackenzie passed over remained remote long after his time. In 1862–1864, there were several Indian massacres of parties of prospectors on the trail that led out of the Bella Coola valley. The area just north of Mackenzie's track was first explored as late as 1892–1904, by an Oblate priest, Father Morice.

p. 139 Keats had yet to publish his lines on Cortes—it was actually Balboa—first gazing upon the Pacific.

p. 141 Missing Mackenzie's Rock. A similar navigational error is described in *The Complete Wilderness Paddler,* page 102.

p. 143 "I had now determined my [latitude and longitude]." This was Mackenzie's definitive position on the voyage, recorded with a flourish as "128.2 W; 52.21.33 N by artificial horizon, 52.20.48 N by natural horizon." But he subsequently gave the position (in letters dated Sept. 10, 1794, and November 17, 1794, and in an undated note at Britain's National Maritime Museum), as 128.15 W and 53.23 N. To further confuse matters, when he published his book, in 1801, the map Mackenzie used showed Cascade Inlet, where he had made the observations, to be east of longitude 128 W. Vancouver's own errors may have contributed to this. (See Note to p. 161, The Crossing of North America.)

DAY TWENTY-EIGHT

p. 147 Zero-zero. Visibility, and ceiling of clouds, in feet.

p. 147 Salmon. See: Van Dyk, "Long Journey of the Pacific Salmon." *National Geographic,* July 1990. 1989 was the best year ever for the salmon catch in all the countries of the Pacific rim. It amounted to nine hundred thousand tons, of which about thirty percent came from salmon farming, however. Meanwhile, salmon runs on the Columbia and Snake rivers are down from eleven million fish in the early part of the century to about two million now.

DAY TWENTY-NINE

p. 148 Vancouver had his work cut out for him in surveying this broken coast. The actual survey work was mostly conducted from two twenty-foot cutters, carried by the larger sailing ships, the *Discovery* and the *Chatham.*

p. 150 . . . an event of sorts: the end of the old forest. . . . The coastal slopes of the Northwest, receiving up to 160 inches of rain in a year, support the remnants of a rain forest of huge trees. The most important species, going south from Alaska, are the Sitka spruce, the western red cedar and the hemlock, the Douglas fir, and finally—in California—the stupendous groves of coast redwood.

> Originally the Pacific Forest covered seventy thousand square miles of Canada and the United States. These are the oldest and largest trees in the world. About sixty percent of Canada's forest has now been destroyed, mostly in the past forty years. In the United States, less than ten percent survives. Conservationists estimate that these forests will be gone in twenty years. Government and timber industry officials disagree; they say it will be fifty to eighty years before the

forests are exterminated. (Catherine Caufield. "The Pacific Forest."
The New Yorker, May 14, 1990)

THE RETURN

p. 153 September 10. . . . Mackenzie doesn't give the exact date of his return. The quotation at the chapter heading is from the journal entry for August 24, the date of his return to his winter camp, at the forks of the Peace and Smoky rivers.

THE CROSSING OF NORTH AMERICA

p. 158 Mackenzie's Instruments. Although Mackenzie does not list his instruments, he mentions, at various points in his narrative, a sextant with artificial horizon (levelled with quicksilver), a telescope, an acrometer (chronometer?), a watch, and a compass.

p. 159 Harrison's Prize. Parliament had offered a handsome prize, partly because they thought the specifications impossible to meet. The prize, and its arbiters—the Board of Longitude—were the butts of eighteenth century humorists. When Harrison met the specifications, he found it difficult to collect the prize, and he was finally paid, in 1773, only through the intervention of King George III. (Brown. *The Story of Maps.*)

p. 159 Galileo invented his method of determining longitude in response to a prize offered by the King of Spain. The Spanish King showed no interest in the proposal by Galileo, who nonetheless spent twenty-four years more perfecting his tables. The church discouraged any use of Galileo's researches, and the matter lapsed. Towards the end of the same century, another Italian, Cassini, who was in the service of the King of France, took up Galileo's work and spent another sixteen years on tables predicting the times of eclipse of the satellites of Jupiter. The method of determining longitude by use of these tables called for "a very fussy technique." Also, the method was useless at sea, on a pitching deck; hence the English interest in developing the chronometer. (Brown. *op. cit.*)

p. 159 Problems with chronometers: On February 2, 1793, Mackenzie says, "it froze so hard my watch stopped." And Lamb mentions that Mackenzie "had the misfortune to allow his chronometer to run down on July 1, 1793." (I did not find this in the *Journals*.)

Lewis and Clark used their chronometer and the method of lunar distances independently to determine longitude. They experienced a number of problems with their chronometer, and seem to have relied mainly on celestial observations.

p. 160 Accuracy of Mackenzie's observations. Where Mackenzie had ample time for observations, his longitude errors were:

At Winter Camp	5 miles
At Canoe Island	11 miles

Where he was under stress, and had little time for observations, his errors were greater:

In Peace River Canyon	67 miles
In Dean Channel	25 miles

(See Table 1, p. 161)

Considering his circumstances, Mackenzie's navigation was quite acceptable by the standards of his time. (According to Lamb, it was subsequently found that Vancouver's observations of the coast were virtually all too far to the east, sometimes by 15–20 miles.)

p. 162 Northwest Passage. Samuel Hearne proved there was no Northwest Passage when he walked from Hudson Bay to the Arctic Ocean, in 1771. His account, however, was not published until 1795: *A Journey from Prince of Wales's Fort in Hudson's Bay to the Northern Ocean.*

p. 162 The Lewis and Clark expedition returned on September 23, 1806, after 2½ years away. A summary of their journals was published in 1814, in two volumes, edited by Nicholas Biddle. The entirety of the journals, with the scientific data and atlas which Jefferson had wished to see published, had to wait until 1904.

p. 163 Mackenzie's track not a practical route. In the final phase of the transcontinental fur trail, the route to and from the Pacific was: along the Columbia River from Astoria to Fort Okanagon;

overland to Fort Alexandria, on the Fraser, by way of Kamloops; and along the Fraser to New Caledonia—the fur country above Prince George. Little or no freight went across the Rockies. Fort Vancouver (site of the present town of Vancouver, Washington) shipped furs out by sea. The transcontinental canoe route, in its entirety, was a communications route only.

p. 166 The Columbia. Because the mouth of the Fraser had not been discovered when Mackenzie published his book, he assumed that the river on which he had travelled was the Columbia, and shows it as such on the map in his book. (This map, as Mackenzie acknowledges in his Introduction, was by Arrowsmith, a London cartographer who made the best maps in the world at that time, incorporating the latest explorations. Lewis and Clark confirmed, by a study of Arrowsmith's current map, that the Missouri was the logical passageway to the Columbia.)

p. 166 Mackenzie's subsequent history: He achieved both fame and fortune. He was knighted by King George III; painted by Sir Thomas Lawrence, the most fashionable painter in Europe; and retired early to Scotland, where he married his beautiful cousin.

p. 166 Larger and slower. Lewis and Clark's was a forty-three man expedition, which travelled at half the speed of Mackenzie's party.

p. 168 Queen Charlotte Islands. See: Johnston, "The Queen Charlotte Islands. Homeland of the Haida." *National Geographic,* July 1987. According to a subsequent news report, the Haida have been allowed to preserve fifteen percent of the Islands' ancient forest. The rest is under "sustained yield management" (read "clear cut").

THE SURVIVAL OF THE BEAVER HAT

p. 173 Quote on the "hard and heavy" hat is from Surtees, *Mr. Sponge's Sporting Tour*. (London, 1852)

p. 173 Manufacture of a traditional beaver hat: see *Enc. Brit.*, 11th Edition, 1910. v. 13, p. 60

p. 175 Roy Rogers and Gene Autry. See Rothel, *The Singing Cowboys*. New York: A. S. Barnes, 1978.

THE FUR TRADE

p. 179 Size of the Fur Trade. The fur trade was not only the largest business in Canada, but was equally important in the U.S., where Jacob Astor's American Fur Co. was, with its subsidiaries, the largest commercial organization in the country.

p. 179 Mackenzie's tally of pelts.

	1798 N.W. Co	1986/7 All Canada
Beaver	106,000	500,000[1]
Bear	2,100	2,942
Fox	5,500	90,000
Otter	4,600	20,668
Muskrat	17,000	1,700,000
Marten	32,000	222,674
Mink	1,800	101,561
Lynx	6,000	6,951
Wolverine	600	744
Fisher	1,650	15,021
Racoon	100	139,221
Wolf	3,800	3,316
Wildcat	not shown	1,748

[1]Same number as 1980/1 season.

It has been estimated that the beaver population at the coming of the white man numbered some ten million. The combined annual take of the Hudson's Bay Company and the North West Company seems not to have exceeded, on any continuous basis, a quarter million beaver pelts. The total beaver population could have sustained this harvest, but the trade was greedy: the beaver was almost wiped out by 1930 because the country was stripped bare, segment by segment. (It didn't help that rising prices made it profitable to kill the beaver in the summer, too.) At the eleventh hour, beaver were reintroduced into their old breeding grounds, and a system of trapping was introduced based on harvesting beaver from counted lodges.

MACKENZIE'S INDIANS

p. 191   Oka. Mackenzie refers to Oka as a village of the Iroquois and Algonquins. (Hakluyt Edition of Mackenzie's *Journals*, p. 85)

p. 192   The last of these treaties was made in 1923.

S·O·U·R·C·E·S

PRINCIPAL REFERENCES

Lamb, W. Kaye, ed. *The Journals and Letters of Sir Alexander Mackenzie*. Cambridge, England: University Press, for the Hakluyt Society, 1970.

This edition, with its useful preface, maps, and footnotes, is much to be preferred over the more modest AMS edition cited below, and which I took with me on my trip to the Coast.

Mackenzie, Alexander. *Voyages from Montreal on the River St. Laurence through the Continent of North America to the Frozen and Pacific Oceans in the Years 1789 and 1793 with an Account of the Rise and State of the Fur Trade in that Country* London, 1801. Republished by Allerton Book Co, New York, 1922. 2 vols. Reprinted by AMS Press, New York, in the American Explorers Series, 1973.

Morse, Eric W. *Canoe Routes of the Voyageurs: The Geography and Logistics of the Canadian Fur Trade*. Toronto: Quetico Foundation of Ontario, and St. Paul: Minnesota Historical Society, 1962. (A reproduction of three articles which appeared in the *Canadian Geographic Journal* in May, July and August, 1961.)

———. *Fur Trade Canoe Routes of Canada/Then and Now*. 2d ed. Toronto: University of Toronto Press, 1984.

Transport Canada. *Water Aerodrome Supplement*. 1990 ed. Ottawa: Aeronautical Information Services.

Woodworth, J., and H. Flygare. *Trail Guide: In the Steps of Alexander Mackenzie*. 2d ed. Kelowna, B.C.: The Alexander Mackenzie Trail Association, 1987.

OTHER REFERENCES

Adamson, Jeremy. *The Canadian Landscape.* (Catalogue to an Exhibition.) Washington D.C.: Embassy of Canada, 1990.

Adney, Edwin T., and Howard I. Chapelle. *The Bark Canoes and Skin Boats of North America.* Washington, D.C.: Smithsonian Institution, 1964.

Aircraft Owners and Pilots Association. *Flight Planning Guide to Canada.* Frederick, Md.: AOPA, 1986.

Bigsby, John J. *The Shoe and Canoe, or Pictures of Travel in the Canadas.* 2 vols. London, 1850. Reprinted, New York: Paladin Press, 1969.

Brady, A. J. *A History of Fort Chipewyan.* Athabasca, Alberta: Gregorach Printing Ltd, 1985.

Brown, Loyd A. *The Story of Maps.* Boston: Little, Brown & Co., 1949.

Campbell, M. W. *The North West Company.* Toronto: MacMillan, 1957.

Canada Government. *Canada Year Book.* 1990 ed. Ottawa: Queen's Printer.

Canada Government. *Indian Treaties and Surrenders.* 3 vols. Ottawa: Queen's Printer, 1912.

Caufield, Catherine. "The Ancient Forest." *New Yorker,* May 14, 1990.

Challenge of the Skies. Edmonton: Pukrin's Production House, Ltd., 1981.

Corbett, Bill. "Vanishing Herds." *Canadian Geographic,* June–July 1991.

Davidson, J. W., and J. Rugge. *The Complete Wilderness Paddler.* New York: Vintage Books, 1983.

Dutton, B. *Navigation and Nautical Astronomy.* 7th ed. Annapolis, Md.: USNI, 1942.

Encyclopedia Britannica. 15th ed. 1977. 11th ed. 1910.

Fitzhugh, William W., and Aron Crowell. *Crossroads of Conti-*

nents: *Cultures of Siberia and Alaska.* Washington D.C.: Smithsonian Press, 1988.

Gray, Ralph. "Across Canada by Mackenzie's Track." *National Geographic,* Aug. 1955.

Guidhall Museum of the City of London. *Short Guide to the Collection of Clocks and Watches.* n.d.

Halsey, D., with Diana Landau. *Magnetic North: A Trek Across Canada from the Pacific to the Atlantic by Foot, Dogsled, and Canoe.* San Francisco: Sierra Club Books, 1990.

Hoyt, Erich, and Susan Milius. "New Bird in a Battered Forest." *International Wildlife,* March–April 1991.

Innis, Harold A. *The Fur Trade in Canada.* Toronto: University of Toronto Press, 1956.

Jenness, Diamond. *Indians of Canada.* 7th ed. Ottawa: National Museum of Canada, 1977.

Johnson, Adrian. *America Explored: A Cartographic History of the Exploration of North America.* New York: Viking Press, 1974.

Johnston, Moira. "The Queen Charlotte Islands. Homeland of the Haida." *National Geographic,* July 1987.

Kennedy, Des. "Pulp from the North." *Canadian Geographic,* June–July 1990.

Krotz, Larry. "Dammed and Diverted." *Canadian Geographic* Feb.–Mar. 1991.

Laurier, Sir Wilfred. "The Forests of Canada." *National Geographic,* Sept. 1906.

Lavender, D. *Winner Take All: A History of the Trans-Canada Canoe Trail.* The American Trails Series. Moscow: Univ of Idaho Press, 1977.

Lower, A. R. M. *The North American Assault on the Canadian Forest.* Toronto: The Ryerson Press, 1938.

McCormack, P. A., and R. G. Ironside, eds. *Proceedings of the Fort Chipewyan and Fort Vermilion Bicentennial Conference, Sept 23–25, 1988.* Edmonton: Boreal Institute of Northern Studies, 1990.

McGuffin, G. and J. *Where Rivers Run: A 6,000-Mile Exploration of Canada by Canoe.* Boulder, Colo.: Stone Wall Press, 1988.

McPhee, John. *The Survival of the Bark Canoe.* New York: Warner Books, 1975.

Meinig, W. *The Shaping of America.* vol I. New Haven: Yale Univ. Press, 1986.

Mowat, Farley. *Sea of Slaughter.* New York: Atlantic Monthly Press, 1984.

———. *Canada North.* Boston: Little, Brown, 1967.

Olson, Sigurd. *The Lonely Land.* New York: Knopf, 1961.

———. *The Singing Wilderness.* New York: Knopf, 1957.

Parkman, Francis. *France and England in North America.* 2 vols. New York: Library of America, 1983.

Rothel, David. *The Singing Cowboys.* New York: A. S. Barnes, 1978.

Sheppe, Walter. *First Man West.* Berkeley: Univ. of Calif. Press, 1962.

Steber, Rick. *New York to Nome. The Northwest Passage by Canoe.* Croton-on-Hudson, N.Y.: North River Press, 1987.

Tait, Hugh. *Clocks and Watches.* London: British Museum, 1983.

Tanner, Ogden. *The Canadians.* Alexandria, VA.: Time-Life Books, 1977.

Thwaites, R. G., ed. *Original Journals of the Lewis and Clark Expedition 1804–1806.* 8 vols. New York: Antiquarian Press, 1959.

Vancouver, George. *A Voyage of Discovery to the North Pacific and Round the World.* Edited by W. Kay Lamb. 4 vols. Cambridge, England: The University Press, for the Hakluyt Society, 1984.

Van Dyk, Jere. "Long Journey of the Pacific Salmon." *National Geographic,* July, 1990.

Wilson, J. A. "Gentlemen Adventurers of the Air." *National Geographic,* Nov. 1929.

MAPS AND CHARTS

Map Supplement. "Indians of North America." *National Geographic,* Dec. 1972.

Aeronautical Charts. Canada Map Office. Aeronautical Charts Division. 615 Booth Street, Ottawa, K1A 0E9.

SEAPLANING

Chichester, Francis. *The Lonely Sea and the Sky*. New York: Paragon House, 1990. (First published, London: Hodder & Stoughton, 1964.)

──────. *Ride on the Wind*. New York: Paragon House, 1989. (First published, London: Hamish Hamilton, 1936.)

De Remer, Dale. *Water Flying Concepts*. Grand Forks, N.D.: De Remer, 1989.

Faure, M. *Flying a Floatplane*. Blue Ridge Summit, PA.: Tab Books, 1984.

Frey, Jay J. *How to Fly Floats*. New York: EDO Commercial Corporation, 1972.

Lindbergh, Anne Morrow. *North to the Orient*. New York: Harcourt, Brace & Co., 1935.

Newstrom, Gordon K. *Fly a Seaplane*. Grand Rapids, MN: Minnesota Flyer, 1983.

Rivest, P. *Bush Pilot*. Montreal: Publications Aeroscope, 1988.

I · N · D · E · X

Abbreviations: AB, Alberta; BC, British Columbia; MB, Manitoba; MD, Maryland; NC, North Carolina; ON, Ontario; QC, Quebec; SK, Saskatchewan; WA, Washington.

Adirondack Mountains, 40, 70
Algonkian language, 20
Amisk Lake, 89
Appalachian Mountains, 12
Arctic Lake, 128, 161
Arrowsmith, Aaron, *mapmaker*, 160, 205
Astor, John Jacob, *fur trader*, 206
Athabasca River, 107, 109
Athabasca tar sands, 109

Back River, MD, 4, 6–10, 29, 30–31, 39
Bad River, BC, 128
Balboa, Vasco Nuñez de, *explorer*, 163, 165
Baltimore, 6, 28, 142
Beaver, airplane, xvi, 41
   hat, 47, 173–77, 206
   mammal, 17, 47, 102, 112, 206
Bella Bella, 23, 141
Bella Coola, village, 20, 23, 140
   river, 136–38, 140, 147–48
Bellingham, 151
Bennett Dam, 111, 125, 200
Benson, Carl, *aviator, assists author*, 147, 149

Birds: at Fort Chipewyan, 113; navigation of, 92; osprey, 6, 100; heron, 6, 43; loon, 64; white pelican, 80, 92, 140; eagle, 133, 145, 150; raven, 142
Blackwater River, see West Road River
Boreal forest, 82, 188
Boyes, Roy, *mechanic*, 87
Brereton Lake, 77
British Columbia (BC), 125
Buffalo Narrows, 95, 98–104
Burke Channel, 141

Caldwell, Jack, *aviator*, 121
Campbell River, 150–51
Canada: exploration of, 15, 157–58, 164; author's arrival in, 41; flight service stations, 55, 58, 98, 140, 150; sparsely settled areas, 78, 186; permafrost line, 113; confederation, 70
Canadian Geographic Journal, 188–89, 209
Canadian National Railway, 67
Canadian Pacific Railway, 67, 70, 108

215

Canadian Shield, 67, 70–71, 77, 84, 89, 92, 98
Canoes: design & construction, xvi, xvii, 195; adoption by white man, 15; poling, 20; lining, 17, 126; portaging, xv, 108, 124, 171; sailing, 119; cross-Canada trips, 169–72; speed of, 169, 197
Canoe Island (Fraser River), 161
Cartier, Jacques, *explorer*, 42, 163
Cascade Inlet, 139, 140
Cedar Lake, 82
Champlain, Samuel de, *explorer*, 15
Charlie Lake, 124–25
Chatham, *HMS*, 150
Chichester, Francis, *seaplaner*, 10, 14, 22, 23
Chronometers, 159, 204
Churchill Lake, 23, 98, 100, 102, 107, 188
Churchill River, 89, 95, 98
Clearwater River, 108–109
Coast Mountains, 131, 132
Columbia River, 158, 163, 196
Combe, William, *editor*, 199
Compass, 12, 32, 49, 82, 132, 158
Connecticut River, 31, 33, 40
Cook, Capt. James, *navigator*, 157–59
Cook Inlet, Alaska, 19
Crooked River, 128, 201
Cumberland House, 88
Curtiss, Glenn, *aviation pioneer*, 4

Delaware River, 32
Dean Channel, 139, 140–41, 161
Dean River, 136
Deep River, 48
Denny Island, 141
Discovery, *HMS*, 148
Discovery Passage, 150
Drummondville, QC, 40
Ducette, Charles, *voyageur*, 46, 198

East Haddam, 33, 39
EDO floats, xvii, 4, 11, 30
Edmonton, 120
Egg Island Light, 147, 149
Euchiniko Lake, 132
Eulachon, fish, 132

Fabre, Henri, *seaplane pioneer*, xvi
Finlay River, 125
Fishing industry, at Fort Chip, 112; at Bella Bella, 141–42
Fitzhugh Sound, 147
Flin Flon, 89
Floatplanes: characteristics of, xv–xvii, 4, 7, 9–10, 25, 58, 118
Fog, 57, 143, 148
Footner Lake, 121
Forests, 49, 82, 150, 168, 188–89, 198, 202
Forster, Mike, *seaplaner*, 6–9, 58, 199
Fort Chipewyan: fur trading post & terminus of the Voyageurs' Highway, 17; center for exploration, 18; author's arrival at, 110; description of, 111; fishing at, 112; Mackenzie's base, 110, 112; mistaken location, 157
Fort Coulonge, 48
Fort Frances, 73

Fort Mackinac, 98
Fort McMurray, 81, 98, 109
Fort Paskoyac, see The Pas
Fort St. John, 120
Fort Vermilion, 120, 200
Fort William, 61
Franklin, Sir John, *explorer*, 16, 92, 110, 164
Fraser, Simon, *fur trader and explorer*, 46, 201
Fraser River, xvii, 129, 205
French River, 56
Friday Harbor, 151
Frobisher, Sir Martin, *adventurer*, 16
Frog Portage, 89
Fur Trade: trunk route, 17; organization, 18; museum at Lachine, 47; in North Bay, 54; entrepôt at Fort William, 61–62; early profitability, 62, 179; trade goods, 76; low prices, 54, 102; rivalries, 179–80; pelts taken, 179, 205

Galileo, Galilei, *solves problem of longitude*, 122, 203
Georgian Bay, 56, 170
Grace Lake, 83, 87
Grand Portage, 18, 62

Halsey, David, *canoeist & trekker*, 171
Harrison, John, *watchmaker*, 159, 203
Havre de Grace, MD, 32
Hearne, Samuel, *explorer*, 164, 204
Henderson, NC, 14
High Level, AB, 120, 200
Hudson Bay, 67, 89, 180

Hudson's Bay Company, 67, 88, 108, 110, 124, 180
Hudson River, 33, 40

Icelandic River, 78
Indian Tribes:
  at The Pas, 85
  Algonquins, 199
  Beaver, 192
  Bella Bella, 148
  Bella Coola, 136, 192
  Carrier, 192
  Cree, 40, 85, 100, 111, 113–14, 192
  Chipewyan, 103, 111, 113–14
  Chilcotin, 191
  Choctaw, 98
  Haida, 168, 205
  Hurons, 190
  Iroquois, 43, 199
  Kahnawake, 43
  Mohawk, 42, 190, 191
  Sekani, 192
  Swampy Cree, 85
Indians: trails of, 17, 132; as guides to Mackenzie, 20, 124, 129, 130, 137; hostile to Mackenzie, 143, 147; numbers, 193; present status, 194

Jay's Treaty, 62
Jefferson, Thomas, *U.S. President*, 162, 166
Johnstone Strait, 150
Jolliet, Louis, *explorer*, 15
Jupiter, planet & satellites, 122, 161, 200

Kaministikwia R. (Kam River), 62
Kelly, Ed, *mechanic*, 31, 149

218 · INDEX

Kenora, 74
King Island, 141
Kluskoil Lake, 132

Lachine, 42
Lachine Rapids, 15, 42
Lac du Bois, see Lake of the Woods
Lac Île a la Crosse, 95
Lac la Croix, 67
Lac la Loche, 89, 102
Lac la Pluie, see Rainy Lake
Lac la Ronge, 38, 88, 99, 105
Lacrosse, *ball game,* 98
Lake Athabasca, 17, 95, 107, 110, 129, 199
Lake Champlain, 40
Lake Chickamauga, 12
Lake Huron, 56
Lake Nipissing, 49
Lake Superior, 57, 59
Lake Whatcom, 153
Lake Williston, 125
Lake Winnipeg, 77–78
Lake of the Woods, 74–76
La Loche R, 107
Lamb, W. Kaye, *archivist,* 209
Landry, Joseph, *voyageur,* 46, 198
La Salle, Robert, *explorer,* 43
Laurier, Sir W., *Canadian premier,* 49
Lewis and Clark, *explorers,* 162–63, 166–67, 204–5
Lindbergh, Anne Morrow, *author,* xvii
Lindbergh, Charles, *lone eagle,* 22, 162, 174
Little Current, ON, 56
Little Grand Rapids, MB, 79

Logging, 125–26, 133, 146, 150, 168, 188, 198
Longitude: methods of determining, 158, 203; Pond's errors, 157
Lyell Island, 168

Mackay, Alexander, *accompanies Mackenzie to Pacific,* 20; dies, 196
McGillivray, William, *fur trader,* 62
McGregor River, 129
McGuffin, G. & J., *canoeists,* 170
MACKENZIE, Alexander (1763–1820)
Pacific Expedition (1792/3)
  summary of, 20–21
  guided by Indians, 20, 124, 129, 130, 137
  leaves Fort Chipewyan, 117
  winters on Peace R, 121–23
  arrives at Forks of Peace R, 124
  follows Parsnip R. to its source, 128
  crosses divide at Arctic lake, 128
  wrecks canoe on Bad R, 128
  turns back up Fraser R, 129
  arrives at West Road River, 131
  arrives at Pacific Ocean, 138–39
  inscribes rock, 139
  determines his position in Dean Channel, 143
  returns to Fort Chipewyan, 153
Arctic expedition of, 19, 162
  as author, 16, 160
  career of, 105, 165–66, 205

character of, 16, 166
effect of his traversing the continent, 167–68
goes to London, 158
observations of Jupiter's satellites, 122, 161
stationed at Fort Chipewyan, 19
Mackenzie, Roderic, *fur trader*, 95
Mackenzie, BC, 125
Maligne River, see Sturgeon-weir River
Manitoulin Island, 57, 170
Marquette, Père, *explorer*, 15
Mattawa River, 49
May, Wop, *aviator*, 121
Methye Portage, 107–108
Métis, 85, 86, 111
Michipicoten, 56–57
Missinipi River, see Churchill River
Missouri River, 15, 166–67
Mocksville, NC, seaplane base, 12
Montreal (Mont Royal), 40, 42–43
Morse, Eric, *canoeist*, 17–18, 65, 170
Mount Mackenzie, BC, 136

National Maritime Museum (England), 196
Navigation, 23, 49, 67, 74, 89, 95, 141, 201
Nelson River, 188
North Battleford, SK, 99
North Bay, 52
North Bentinck Arm, 140
Northwest Passage, 16, 162, 164, 204

North West Company, 47, 88, 164, 180
Nuñez Cabez de Vaca, *goldseeker*, 165

Oka, QC, 42, 191, 199
Olson, Sigurd, *outdoorsman*, 71, 193, 198
Ottawa River, 48
Ottawa City, 49
Otter, airplane, xvi, 78, 104
  mammal, 54, 201, 206

Pacific Lake, 128
Pacific Ocean, goal of early explorers, 15; reached by Mackenzie, 138
Pack River, 126, 201
Parsnip River, 126
Pays d'en haut, 49, 180
Pays Plat, ON, 59
Peace River, 19, 111, 118–25, 153
Pelechaty, Bruce, *prevents accident*, 84
Peter Pond Lake, 102, 107, 108
Piedmont Bible College, NC, 12
Pigeon River (location of Grand Portage), see Map 4
Pinehouse Lake, 95
Pine Island Light, 147
Pointe au Baptême, 49
Pond, Peter, *fur trader & explorer*, 19, 88, 104, 116, 157
Pope, Jeff, *canoeist*, 169
Portage du Rat, see Kenora
Portage de Traite, see Frog Portage
Port Alberni, BC, 188
Port Hardy, BC, 146, 150
Prince George, BC, 125–26

Queen Charlotte, ship, 168
  Islands, 168
  Sound, 148
Quetico-Superior, 23, 198

Rainy Lake, 53, 67, 73
Rainy River, 67, 73
Rat Portage, see Kenora
RCMP (Royal Canadian Mounted Police), 101–102
Rendezvous Lake, 108
Richelieu River, 40
Riverton, MB, 77–80, 82
Roberts, Wayne, *aviator*, 56, 58
Rocky Mountains: as barrier, 19; first seen by Mackenzie, 123; crossed by Mackenzie, 167; crossed by Lewis & Clark, 167
Rupert's Land, 67

Ste. Anne de Belleville, 43, 197
St. Francis River, 40, 48
St. Lawrence River, 15, 40, 42–43, 47–48
Salmon fishery, 147–48, 202
San Juan Islands, 151
Saskatchewan River, 15, 83–84, 87
Sault Ste. Marie, 57
Seaplanes, see Floatplanes
Seattle, 145
Shearwater, BC, 141
Shovell, Sir Cloudsley, *makes fatal longitude error*, 158
Small Lake, 21, 110, 117–18
Smoky River, 20, 121
Souchuk, Peter, *trekker*, 171
Spinelli, Charles, *aviator*, 5
Squaw Rapids, 89, 199

Strait of Georgia, 146
Stupendous Mountain, BC, 131, 137
Sturgeon-weir River, 89
Summit Lake, 128
Susquehanna River, 32

Tabor Lake, 126, 130–31, 156
Tanya Lakes, 136
Taylor, Shell, *canoeist*, 169
The Pas, 76, 83
Thompson, David, *explorer*, 70, 163
Thunder Bay, 59–61, 63–64, 67, 84
Trout Lake, 48–49
Tsacha Lake, 132

Vancouver, Capt. George, *navigator*, 141, 159, 160, 202
Vancouver, WA, 205
Vancouver Island, BC, 140, 145, 188
Verendrye, Pierre de la, *explorer*, 15
Vermilion Chutes, 119
Victoria, BC, 70
Voyageurs, 15, 46, 53, 62, 75, 88
Voyageurs' Highway, 17, 67, 71, 76, 88, 89

Waglisla, BC, 141
Wa Wa, ON, 55, 57
Water Aerodrome Supplement, 22, 59
West Road River, 131
Williston Lake, 125
Winnipeg River, 77
Wood Buffalo National Park, 118